container
Gardening

By Vicki Webster and the Editors of Sunset Books, Menlo Park, California

Crazy About Containers

It's no secret that in recent years container gardening has steadily grown in popularity. Faced with shrinking outdoor space, people are building entire mini-landscapes that have all their roots in pots. Basic gardening techniques are the same whether you have one plant or several dozen, but when your garden is growing in containers, it has a limited amount of space, soil, and nutrients, and much more is involved in its care. This book presents the practical aspects of designing and tending a container garden and also provides inspiration for creating your personal paradise—atop a city roof, on a suburban patio or deck, or in a window box.

We would like to thank the following people for their assistance with this book: Steven C. Baumhoff, Alan Bendotoff, Donna Bendotoff, Linda Bouchard, Marion Brenner, Kathleen Brenzel, Julie Carman, John Carman, Scott Daigre, Teena Garay, John Glover, Eileen Isola, Rick LaFrentz, Cathy Mann, Rod Mann, Walt McAllister, Judy Robertson, Phoebe Rowles, Hilda Schwerin, Jill Slater, Robert John Smith, Laura Stern, Thomas J. Story, Bud Stuckey, Danuta Szefler, Marian Szefler, John Trager of the Huntington Botanical Gardens, and Brian Vocker.

SUNSET BOOKS

VICE PRESIDENT, GENERAL MANAGER
Richard A. Smeby
VICE PRESIDENT, EDITORIAL DIRECTOR
Bob Doyle
PRODUCTION DIRECTOR
Lory Day
OPERATIONS DIRECTOR
Rosann Sutherland
RETAIL SALES DEVELOPMENT MANAGER
Linda Barker
EXECUTIVE EDITOR
Bridget Biscotti Bradley
ART DIRECTOR
Vasken Guiragossian

STAFF FOR THIS BOOK

MANAGING EDITOR
Claudia Blaine
SENIOR GARDEN EDITOR, SUNSET BOOKS
Marianne Lipanovich
WRITER
Vicki Webster
COPY EDITOR
Barbara J. Braasch
ART DIRECTOR
Vasken Guiragossian
PHOTOGRAPHY EDITOR
Caren Alpert
PHOTOGRAPHY STYLIST
Jill Slater
ILLUSTRATOR
Tracy La Rue Hohn
PAGE PRODUCTION
Joan Olson
PREPRESS COORDINATOR
Danielle Javier
PROOFREADER
Elissa Rabellino
INDEXER
Nanette Cardon

Cover photography by Thomas J. Story; container design by Jill Slater.

15 14 13 12 11 10
First printing January 2004
Copyright © 2004
Sunset Publishing Corporation,
Menlo Park, CA 94025.
Sixth edition. All rights reserved, including the right of reproduction in whole or in part in any form. Library of Congress Control Number: 2003109782. ISBN: 0-376-03208-1. Printed in the United States of America.

For additional copies of *Container Gardening* or any other Sunset book, call 1-800-526-5111 or visit us at *www.sunsetbooks.com*

contents

CHAPTER ONE

The Basics

THE PRACTICE OF GROWING PLANTS *in pots is almost as old as human civilization. But in the past decade or so, container gardening has soared to new heights of popularity. The reasons are many. Gardening has become the country's number one leisure pastime, and potting up a few geraniums or petunias gives novices an easy and inexpensive way to test the waters. Interest in outdoor decor is on the rise, and beautiful plants paired with carefully chosen pots enhance any setting. ❧ Then there are simple demographics: For more and more Americans, the only "land" they have to call their own is a balcony, a rooftop, or a courtyard with a few square feet of planting beds. The popularity of container gardening has given rise to countless books that explain the techniques of choosing, planting, and tending plants in pots. This book goes one step beyond and shows you how to design, grow, and care for a garden that just happens to be in containers.*

Tall, simple terra-cotta pots are a perfect match for these dramatic-looking— and unthirsty—succulents.

Choosing Containers

Whether you garden on a rooftop high above a big city or tend a few pots on the porch of a country cottage, the key to beautiful, thriving container plants is simple: plenty of tender loving care. Plants growing in containers are in an artificial environment, with a finite amount of soil from which to draw water and nutrients and little to protect their roots from drying winds, scorching sun, or freezing cold.

FIRST STEPS

That concept may sound daunting, but the reality needn't be. It simply means that to ensure success, you'll want to give your plants the best possible growing conditions right from the beginning. The process starts with choosing containers that suit your plants and your site.

In one sense, when it comes to selecting containers for your garden, the only limits are your taste and imagination. After all, a plant will send out roots in anything that holds soil, from a custom-crafted alabaster urn to a cast-off bathtub. From a practical standpoint, though, your choice of containers is more than a matter of style; it can determine how well your garden will grow and how much time and attention you will have to give it.

SIZE AND SHAPE

When selecting a container, keep in mind the mature size, growth rate, and root structure of the plants you intend to put in it. It's crucial that a pot be neither too

ABOVE: *This softly mounded planting of verbena and rose vervain (Verbena canadensis) complements its rounded pot.* RIGHT: *Any plant would make a strong statement in this classically inspired pot.*

A garden of lavender and a table for two lend Mediterranean flair to this tiny balcony.

big nor too small. Without ample room to spread, a plant's roots quickly exhaust the nutrients and oxygen in the soil.

On the other hand, in a container that is too large, rapid growers may put out too much leaf growth, which delays and can even prevent flowering and fruiting. When slowly growing plants are put in quarters that are too big, the roots cannot fully permeate the soil, which—except perhaps in a very warm

climate—stays cold and wet. Eventually the soil turns sour, inviting fungus, diseases, and other root problems.

Shape, too, is important for plants' health as well as simple aesthetics. For example, spring crocuses, with their shallow roots and short top growth, will look good and perform well in a pot that's only a few inches high. On the other hand, dill, with its tall foliage and long taproots, needs a container that's deep enough to

accommodate the roots without their bending and also visually balance the upper portion.

How does "big enough" translate into specific measurements? That's where growth rate comes into play. Often a rampant grower such as mint will fill a seemingly too-large container very quickly. As a general rule, though, plants perform their best when you allow about 1 inch of space all the way around the root ball.

MATERIALS

Although improvised containers can be made of anything under the sun, the pots most commonly available commercially are made of terra-cotta, wood, or plastic. Each type has advantages and disadvantages. Which one will work best in your garden depends on your climate, the style of your house, and the time and inclination you have for garden maintenance.

TERRA-COTTA IS ...

Porous. That keeps soil from getting soggy—a very useful feature in cool, rainy, or humid climates—but it does necessitate frequent watering. Salts and minerals are wicked outward and collect on the pot, not in the soil. That's good for plants' health but does cause white stains on pots.

Heavy. That provides for stability—a big plus for trees and tall shrubs, or any plants in a windy location. On the downside, a large pot filled with soil is difficult to move and may be too heavy to use on a rooftop or balcony.

Fragile. Top-quality, high-fired pots are more durable than their mass-produced, low-fired counterparts, but all terra-cotta can chip, crack, and break. Except in very mild climates, clay containers need winter protection. Where winter weather is severe, pots are safest indoors.

These ornamental cabbages, in their terra-cotta pot, will need plenty of water.

WOOD IS ...

Porous (maybe). Untreated wood is somewhat breathable, but wooden containers that have been treated with waterproof paint or other sealer become nonporous.

Naturally insulating. Potting mix remains at a fairly even temperature in a wooden container, as long as the walls are at least ⅞ inch thick.

Durable. Wooden containers can be remarkably long-lived if they're made of rot-resistant redwood, cedar, or cypress. Other woods can be treated to last a long time. Wood rarely breaks, cracks, or chips, and it's not greatly affected by changes in the weather.

Plastic pots (above) come in shapes that echo those of stone containers (left).

PLASTIC IS ...

Nonporous. Water remains in the soil longer—a big plus if you live in a hot, dry climate or want to grow plants that love moisture. In a wet climate, however, or in the case of plants that need drier soil, plastic can be a big drawback.

Noninsulating. Plastic provides little protection from heat or cold. To keep plants safe from temperature extremes, it's best to set plastic pots inside other insulating containers.

Lightweight. On the plus side, that means plastic will work where other materials might be too heavy. But it also means that in a windy or exposed location, plastic pots need to be anchored to the ground or set inside heavier containers.

Durable (maybe). Better-quality plastics are not prone to weather damage, but less expensive versions tend to crack after a few years in the sun and become brittle in the cold.

Salvia and rosemary prefer soil on the dry side, so these unsealed wooden planters are ideal for them.

Not-So-Ordinary Containers

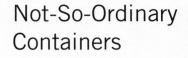

Some of the best containers were never designed to hold plants at all. Take these, for instance: part of an old stone pillar (top), a venerable chimney pot (middle), and a shiny new horse trough (bottom). For these and other winners, check antiques and thrift stores, architectural salvage yards, and farm-supply dealers.

Drainage

Waterlogged soil is the most common cause of death for container plants. The simplest way to avoid the problem is to use free-draining planting mix and make sure that each pot has at least one opening in the bottom to expel excess water. If you fall in love with a container that has no drainage hole, don't despair—you do have options.

DRILL A HOLE

Use either a hand or electric drill for wood, plastic, or fiberglass. For stone, terra-cotta, or concrete, use an electric drill with a masonry or carbide bit. (To avoid cracking the pot, drill a small hole first and increase the bit size to a larger one.) Heavy lead or iron containers

You can use an electric drill with either a carbide or masonry bit to make drainage holes in terra-cotta, stone, or concrete pots.

require the use of a metal bit, but for lighter ones, such as buckets or decorative tins, you can easily punch holes with a hammer and large nail. A single ½- to 1-inch hole will suffice for small- to medium-size containers. For larger ones, such as half-barrels, drill four or five 1-inch holes.

DOUBLE-POT

If drilling is not an option, plant in a smaller container that has drainage holes and set it inside the solid one. Just be sure to raise the inner pot on bricks or pebbles so that it never sits in water. Size permitting, it's also a good idea to remove the inner pot from time to time and empty any water that has accumulated at the bottom of the outer container.

Before you plant, test your double-pot combo for size. Set the inner, draining pot on bricks or pebbles so that it reaches just below the rim of the outer container.

SAY NO TO SHARDS

At planting time, ignore the traditional advice to cover your containers' drainage holes with pot shards. New studies show that rather than improving drainage, they can actually hinder it. Instead, put a small square of window screening over each opening in the bottom. It will keep soil in the pot but still allow water to drain out.

Nurseries and garden shops sell terracotta pots in countless styles, sizes, and price ranges. Most come equipped with drainage holes, which will spare you drilling time and effort.

Set Them Up

One way to promote good drainage and increase air circulation—as well as prevent water stains on decks and patios—is to lift containers off the ground. You can buy pot "feet" for just that purpose (the lions in the photo at right are one example), but wood blocks, bricks, or small overturned flower pots work just as well. Other ways and means: nail cleats to the bottoms of wooden containers, or look for pots with built-in risers.

Potting Mixes

It might seem that good topsoil, straight from the garden, should work fine in your pots. Not so. Even the best loam is too dense to use by itself in containers. It's possible to combine garden soil with other additives to get the right combination of fast drainage and rich nutrition that container plants need. But there's no reason to bother when many high-quality mixes are available.

Standard potting mix, either peat- or soil-based, works fine for most plants.

HOW MUCH POTTING MIX?

Whether you're potting a basket of petunias for the summer or planting a container garden filled with long-lived trees, shrubs, and perennials, there are ready-made mixes to suit your needs (and those of your plants).

While potting mix is generally sold by the cubic foot, standard containers are usually labeled by inches. Listed below are some helpful translations.

A 2-cubic-foot bag of potting mix is enough to fill

- eight to ten standard 10- to 12-inch pots;
- two pots 12 inches in diameter and 15 inches deep;
- one window box or planter that measures 36 by 8 by 10 inches.

SOIL OR SOILLESS?

Most garden centers carry a bewildering array of potting mixes, but they all fall into one of two broad categories: soil-based or soilless. As the name implies, soil-based mixes contain real, garden-variety loam (sterilized, of course) along with varying amounts of plant food and additives such as peat, sand, bark chips, vermiculite, or per-

lite. Soil-based mixes are heavier than soilless versions, and they tend to be messier to use. On the plus side, they retain water and nutrients better and provide greater stability for plants. They are by far the better choice for plants that will stay in the same pots for more than a year or so.

Soilless mixes are based on peat or a peat substitute such as coir, which is made from shredded and composted coconut husks. Depending on the formulation, these mixes contain the same kinds of additives you'll find in the soil-based types. Soilless mixes dry out and lose nutrients fairly rapidly, but their light weight and ease of handling make them ideal for hanging baskets and annual plantings of all kinds.

GETTING SPECIFIC

For most plants a general-purpose potting mix, either soil-based or soilless, will work just fine. For others, you'll want to use a special formulation. When in doubt, don't guess about which kind to use; consult with the nursery staff when you purchase your plants, and be sure to mention any requirements specific to your site, such as lightweight or good

water retention. Here are some of the most common specialty potting mixes.

AQUATIC PLANT MIX A heavy, viscous, soil-based mix designed to stay in place when pots are submerged in water.

CACTI AND SUCCULENT MIX A mixture of soil, sand, and peat or peat substitute, with gravel or other grit added to ensure excellent drainage.

ERICACEOUS MIX A must for acid-loving plants such as azaleas, camellias, and rhododendrons. Most brands are peat-based, with no lime added to neutralize the peat's natural acid.

CONTAINER AND HANGING-BASKET MIXES Peat-based formulas with both water-retaining gel crystals and slow-release fertilizer gran-

Planting with Polymers

Water-retaining gel crystals absorb hundreds of times their weight in water, making them a real boon to container gardeners. Mixed into the soil, these superabsorbent polymers hold on to both water and dissolved nutrients, keeping them readily available to plant roots. That's a particular advantage for hanging baskets or for pots in hot climates or exposed sites where containers dry out quickly. You can buy commercial potting mixes with gel already added, but mixing it yourself is simple. Just remember that no matter how dry or windy your garden site, more is not better; follow package instructions precisely. An overdose of gel will keep the soil too wet, which could kill your plants.

1

Sprinkle the dry crystals into water and stir until they swell up to form a thick gel. The package will tell you the correct proportion of crystals to water.

2

Pour your potting mix into a wheelbarrow or other large container and add the bloated crystals to the potting mix.

3

Using gloved hands or a trowel, combine the crystals with your potting mix. Again, follow the package directions for the ratio of crystals to soil.

4

Once you've thoroughly combined the potting mix and crystals, put the gel-laced soil in your pots and plant in the normal way.

ules added. These mixes save time and labor, but they are expensive. If you have more than a few containers to fill and your budget is a factor, you'll be better off buying crystals and fertilizer separately and adding them to a standard potting mix. (See "Planting with Polymers" above.)

In order to thrive, any container plant needs regular supplies of water and fertilizer. Even potting mixes with food added have to be replenished eventually. Read the bag carefully so that you'll know when to start supplementary feedings.

CHAPTER TWO

Entryways

ANY BEAUTIFUL ENTRANCE GARDEN offers a festive greeting to guests, delights passersby, and welcomes you home in style after a long, hard day—or even a short, easy one. An entry garden in containers does more than that: it provides the makings of an ever-changing "welcome mat," letting you create a new floral greeting with each passing season or whim. The display needn't be large or elaborate to be effective. A simple window box or a hanging basket beside a doorway will catch eyes, lift spirits, and enhance your home's architecture. Of course, along with the joy of creating a work of living art for all the world (or at least all your neighborhood) to see comes a challenge: keeping that showplace looking good throughout the year.

Containers of nasturtiums (Tropaeolum), *foxgloves* (Digitalis purpurea), *and geraniums usher guests up these stairs in colorful style.*

Year-Round Appeal

In places where mild weather reigns throughout the year, keeping your entry garden in top form is pretty straightforward. Simply find plants that please you and suit your growing conditions; give them good, basic care (see pages 103–125); and replace them when they outgrow their pots or when you want a change of scene. In most parts of the country, though, it helps to have a few tricks up your sleeve.

KEEP IT SIMPLE

It can be tempting to deck your entryway with the beautiful, multiplant creations you see in magazines and in this book. It is a satisfying way to let your creative juices flow, especially if an entryway is the only planting space you have.

But remember that the more complex a planting is, the more care and attention you will have to give it, and the greater are the chances that something will go awry and spoil the arrangement. (After all, plants are living organisms, not decorative objects.) For the ultimate in easy good looks,

plant one or, at most, two varieties per container. Then, for instance, when your tulips pass their prime, black spot befalls your miniature roses, or a heat wave flattens your pansies, it takes only minutes to whisk the victims out of sight and bring in healthier replacements.

BELOW LEFT: *'Blue Delft' hyacinths and tiny 'Tête-à-Tête' narcissus march up a stairway. This no-fuss-no-muss display is easy to care for and a snap to change with the seasons.*

BELOW: *An ivy geranium (Pelargonium peltatum) forms a fluffy pink cloud on an entry ledge.*

LEFT: *The lush foliage of scented geraniums, ornamental grasses, and succulents keep this entry looking fresh and inviting. From a distance, the arrangement looks more like an in-ground bed than a cluster of pots.*

BELOW LEFT: *The ultimate in simple welcomes: a basket of variegated English ivy* (Hedera helix) *hung on a door. To achieve a similar visual effect with an aromatic bonus, you could substitute a trailing herb such as creeping thyme* (Thymus serpyllum) *or Corsican mint* (Mentha requienii).

BELOW: *Pots of golden-leafed hosta glow like beacons, pointing the way through a hidden garden to the entrance of the house.*

FOCUS ON FOLIAGE

Foliage plants supply structure, form, and long-lasting good looks. Choose plants that pack a dramatic, leafy punch on their own, such as coleus, ornamental grasses, and hostas. Or use more subtle foliage like that of ferns, boxwood, and ivy as a backdrop for colorful flowers. For a display that pleases the nose as well as the eye, add herbs with aromatic foliage such as mint, scented geraniums, basil, and artemisia. Bear in mind, though, that your climate will determine whether even the hardiest plants can grace your entry all year long.

A Matter of Style

The most successful container gardens bring out the best features of the houses they accompany. And though it may sound overly dramatic, the effect achieved at the entrance can make or break the scheme. After all, that is where people get their first glimpse of your home, and in the words of countless mothers and high school guidance counselors, you get only one chance to make a good first impression.

HARMONY OR HISTORY?

There are two basic approaches to blending house and garden. Some gardeners strive to replicate period gardens that are authentic to the tiniest detail. If you live in a historic or architecturally significant house and have a penchant for the past, you may want to pick up a book on the subject. Like container gardening, period gardening is growing in popularity throughout the country. If you're like most gardeners, though, chances are you just want to create beautiful surroundings that harmonize with the house. Whichever of these camps you fall into, containers add one more element to your design palette.

TOP: *A rustic stuccoed house with a Mediterranean feel meets its match in this low-key yet sophisticated planting. A tall terra-cotta jar, with a palm in the center, echoes the strong vertical lines of the doorway.*

LEFT: *Color and structure make this entry garden a standout. The architectural shapes of succulents complement the simple lines of the house, while the red tones of coleus play off its adobe-colored walls.*

ABOVE: *An entryway that is as unpretentious as this one calls for an equally down-home planting scheme. Simple terra-cotta pots of geraniums, petunias, pansies, and nasturtiums fill the bill perfectly. Note that the pots are set as close as possible to the stair rail, allowing free passage up and down the steps. (For more tips on stairway container gardens, see page 22.)*

LEFT: *The pale shingled wall of an old-fashioned porch forms the perfect backdrop for a pair of blue ceramic pots filled with equally old-fashioned blooms. Given basic care, these trouble-free performers will strut their stuff all summer long. The cast includes geraniums, petunias, sweet alyssum* (Lobularia maritima), *common heliotrope* (Heliotropium arborescens), *and daisies.*

19

ABOVE: *In the entry to this contemporary Asian-influenced house, pots of ornamental grasses and huge specimen hostas hold their own against the striking architecture.*

LEFT: *To accent the stylish door, a single well-designed container features curly straw-colored sedge, along with the hot tones and multiple layers of zinnias, strawflowers* (Helichrysum bracteatum), *petunias, and geraniums.*

FACING PAGE, TOP: *'Barbara Karst' bougainvillea, Russian sage* (Perovskia atriplicifolia), *and woolly thyme* (Thymus pseudolanuginosus) *help pull off this entryway's Mediterranean theme.*

FACING PAGE, BOTTOM: *A lead planter echoes the symmetrical lines of a formal doorway. Red geraniums, purple violas, and blue lobelia add a splash of color.*

Think "Bones"

Attractive containers and accessories can do for a potted garden what well-shaped trees and shrubs do for an in-ground landscape: provide lasting interest (what garden designers call "bones") long after flowers and leaves have fallen.

To put that principle to work in your entryway, top a stunning container with an equally eye-catching support system and plant a flowering vine at its base. Foliage and flowers will cloak the support throughout the growing season. When the plant dies back, the architectural framework will remain. At that time you can choose to leave it bare or deck it with trimmings of your choice, such as evergreen boughs and twinkling lights.

Stairs and Walkways

A container garden can turn a ho-hum sidewalk or set of stairs into a magical passageway, luring you onward with color and scent. As with any garden, the first key to success is choosing plants that thrive in your climate and setting, and giving them good care. The second lies in remembering one major fact: this garden will not simply be looked at, it will be walked through—possibly run, skipped, and romped through—on a regular basis.

CLOSE QUARTERS

A designer's rule of thumb says that the ideal walk or stairway leading to a house measures at least 4 feet wide, the minimum space needed to give two or three people room to stroll comfortably. But in real life, many of us are not blessed with that much room. That doesn't mean you have to abandon your dreams of a verdant passageway; just allow as much space as possible and take a few basic precautions to ensure the safety of people, pets, and plants. Some, or all, of the following measures will help.

AVOID FRAGILE CONTAINERS

Setting a terra-cotta pot beside a narrow path or on a steep set of stairs is asking for trouble. Instead, look for attractive containers made of unbreakable materials such as wood, metal, or sturdy plastic. And steer clear of narrow, top-heavy shapes that can tip over.

KEEP PLANTS LOW When space is tight, use compact, low-growing plants. They are far less likely to be damaged or to fall over than trees, shrubs, and trellised plants.

DON'T GO LIGHT The heavier a pot is, the less likely it will be to topple if someone, or some lawn tool, bumps into it. Choose the biggest, weightiest containers your space and budget will allow. Then, to both increase stability and conserve potting mix, use a variation of the pot-lightening technique described on page 78. Once you've placed your containers at their final sites, fill the bottom 8 inches or so with rocks. (Use this trick only with annuals and shallow-rooted perennials, not for trees and shrubs; the latter two plantings need all the root room they can get.)

CLAMP DOWN If your garden rests on a wooden stairway or boardwalk, fasten containers to the surface. Whenever possible, attach planters to railings so that they hang outside of the walking area.

ABOVE LEFT: *The lesson to be learned from this delightful stairway garden: if you've got it, flaunt it. Here, galvanized-metal pails, kettles, pots, and watering cans keep culinary herbs within easy clipping distance—and provide a welcome that no guest is likely to forget.*

LEFT: *An urban entrance provides a textbook example of savvy stairway design. Narcissus-filled pots all but shout "Happy Spring!" now, but when their glory has faded, they'll be easy to whisk away and replace with summer annuals. Their location, outside the stair rails, puts them beyond reach of hurrying feet. As further insurance, the pots are plastic—unlikely to break in the event of a fall.*

ABOVE: *Large, heavy pots deliver visual substance and are unlikely to topple if a guest or a pet bumps into them. The plants, which include common yarrow (Achillea millefolium), purple coneflower (Echinacea purpurea), Coreopsis grandiflora, and Mexican bush sage (Salvia leucantha), hold their own against the adobe wall.*

LEFT: *When you set containers along a busy walkway, keep the center of gravity low. These stout pots, filled with mounding petunias and twinspur (Diascia), are more stable than they would be filled with taller plants.*

A Fragrant Welcome

Research has shown that of the five senses, smell is the one fully developed at birth. It is also the one most closely tied to memory—which explains why the faintest whiff of lilacs might send your mind racing back to your grandmother's garden. So why not tap into the power of scent to create a container garden that will linger in your guests' minds for years to come?

BEFORE

Fragrant red miniature roses flank an eye-stopping pot of dahlias and blanket flower (Gaillardia × grandiflora 'Burgundy'). The scent of hedge lavender (Lavandula × intermedia 'Provence') wafts from the background.

On the stairs, a one-two punch of geraniums: salmon-pink common geraniums (Pelargonium × hortorum) in front, backed up by lemon-scented P. 'Atomic Snowflake'.

BEAUTIFUL BECOMES BETTER

Even unadorned, this stunning entryway offered a gracious welcome to guests and to the family that lives here. Now it makes every arrival both festive and memorable, thanks to a container garden that focuses on color, form, texture, and fragrance.

FACING PAGE, BOTTOM: *To the right of the doorway a cluster of pots captivate the eye and nose alike. The intensely fragrant standard rose 'Charisma' stands tall, underplanted with red miniature roses. A mixed planting of lantana, yarrow, and kangaroo paw (Anigozanthos) complements a bowl-shaped terra-cotta pot. The container on the top step emits the blended aromas of pineapple sage and lavender. To the left of the doorway, the lavender and rose scents repeat, joined by the smells of a dwarf citrus tree and lemon-scented geraniums on the steps.*

Fragrance Is Back

For a while, fragrant flowers all but disappeared from the nursery trade as hybridizers focused on bigger, showier blossoms and a wider color range. Unfortunately, most often that visual drama came at the expense of scent. But in recent years, fragrant gardens have gained favor. As a result, nurseries and catalogs offer an increasing number of aromatic plants every year. The list below offers some good choices.

Angel's trumpet (*Brugmansia*)
Chocolate cosmos (*Cosmos atrosanguineus*)
Common heliotrope (*Heliotropium arborescens*)
English lavender (*Lavandula angustifolia*)
Freesia
Hosta plantaginea 'Aphrodite'
Mint (*Mentha*)
Oriental lily (*Lilium* Oriental hybrids such as 'Rosy Dawn', 'Lush Life', 'Stargazer', or 'Black Beauty')
Petunia × hybrida **(Not all petunias are fragrant, so sniff before you buy!)**
Pineapple sage (*Salvia elegans* or *S. elegans* 'Honey Melon Sage')
Pink (*Dianthus*)
Scented geranium (*Pelargonium*)
Shining jasmine (*Jasminum laurifolium nitidum*)
Stock (*Matthiola incana*)
Sweet alyssum (*Lobularia maritima*)
Sweet azalea (*Rhododendron arborescens*)
Sweet olive (*Osmanthus fragrans*)
Sweet pea (*Lathyrus odoratus*)

CHAPTER THREE

Decks and Porches

A WELL-DESIGNED DECK OR PORCH can add character and charm to any home. But these structures are far more than simply architectural appendages. Physically and psychologically, decks and porches bridge the space between indoors and out. And they perform that task much more smoothly with the help of plants in containers. ❧ *Whether that means perching a few window boxes on the railings, adding colorful pots to tables, or installing a potted herbaceous border around the perimeter depends on your taste and how you plan to use the space. For instance, will your portable garden serve as a warm-weather living room, a play area for active children, or simply a quiet place to sit, sip, and watch the world go by? However you want your outdoor room to function, a well-planned container garden will enrich the hours you spend there.*

Bright red Adirondack chairs, arranged for easy conversation, and big color-filled pots transform this deck into an outdoor room. A strawberry jar puts pick-your-own treats just a short reach away.

A Gallery of Decks and Porches

Regardless of its style or purpose, a deck or porch really comes into its own when you add a container garden. It is important, however, that the container plantings complement the structure, thrive in your climate zone, and suit both your taste and your inclination for plant tending. In the gallery of photographs that follows, you'll find plenty of inspiration to start you on the road to satisfying these various criteria.

FACING PAGE, TOP: *A bare-bones deck gets a lift from a prairie-style arrangement of ornamental grasses and meadow flowers, including gloriosa daisy* (Rudbeckia hirta) *and—spilling over the edge—black-eyed Susan vine* (Thunbergia alata).

RIGHT: *This upper-deck container garden features resilient plants that can handle sea breezes and salt spray, such as blanket flower* (Gaillardia × grandiflora) *and Santa Barbara daisy* (Erigeron karvinskianus).

ABOVE: *A brick-paved porch becomes one with the backyard beyond, thanks to careful plant selection. Standard roses and pots of bright annuals echo the tones of the plantings in the rest of the yard.*

LEFT: *A lush container garden brings life to the sedate tones of a second-story deck. Flowers contrast with the monotone gray of house, deck, and railing, but the space retains a peaceful and relaxed feeling. The secret is a well-planned color scheme of mostly green and white, with splashes of yellow and hot pink.*

ABOVE: *Symmetry is the name of the game here. A quartet of identical containers has been painted to match the gray color of the house and deck. Inside the pots, look-alike plantings with flowers in tones of yellow and pink add sparkle without altering the low-key mood.*

LEFT: *When it comes to playing up water views with container plants, there are two schools of thought. One favors cool, aqueous shades of blue, mauve, and lavender that all but melt into the scenery. The other votes for vibrant contrast. This lakeside deck near Seattle clearly falls into the latter category. The eye-popping arrangement includes red geraniums, white marguerites* (Chrysanthemum frutescens), *yellow* Euryops, *purple and white petunias, feathery green parrot beak* (Clianthus puniceus), *deep blue lobelia, ivy, and gray dusty miller.*

RIGHT: *An elegant porch greets spring with a pink, white, and yellow chorus line. When the tulips, daffodils, and primroses (Primula) have gone by the wayside, summer-blooming bulbs and annuals will take their places. Likely candidates are pastel and white lilies against the railing, with lower-growing impatiens and violas below.*

BELOW: *Neatly trained spiral box-wood topiaries, paired with a teak table and chairs, lend a formal air to this dining alcove. If you're tempted to copy the look, be forewarned: you'll have to spend time snipping and clipping to keep the topiaries shipshape.*

RIGHT: *Bordered by columns and bountiful pots of flowers, a long and narrow porch overlooks a Florida canal. This waterside retreat boasts furniture worthy of an indoor living room.*

BELOW: *On a tiny deck in the woods, massed pots of tulips are about to burst into bloom. They'll be white, like the blooms of surrounding trees. Even the cushioned bistro chairs carry out the soothing green and white scheme.*

LEFT: *Here's the ultimate in innovative containers: concrete drainage pipes planted with red impatiens and lit with neon rings. Across the walkway from this offbeat lineup, orange cannas repeat the earth-and-fire-toned theme. Aside from a successful use of color, there's another design lesson to be learned from this container garden: you never know where you'll find a fabulous container—so keep your eyes open and your imagination working overtime.*

RIGHT: *Like many old-time flowers, cannas have enjoyed a resurgence of popularity. They are a perfect choice for sleek blue planters beside an ultra-modern chaise. Also in the planter are coleus, sweet potato vine (Ipomoea batatas), and ornamental grasses.*

33

On the Long and Narrow

When you build a deck or porch from scratch or expand an existing one, you can easily tailor the design to suit your needs and tastes. Often, the much tougher challenge is to define appealing outdoor living areas when the spaces can't be tailored. This is particularly true when a patio or deck is long and narrow, as is often the case. It's then that plants and containers come into their own as architectural elements, helping to delineate space and even fooling the eye.

DIVIDE AND CONQUER

One way to deal with an awkwardly proportioned structure is simply to break it up into smaller areas with more pleasing measurements. By clever arrangement of plants, furniture, and accent pieces, you can create as many separate alcoves as your space will allow. You can establish permanent areas for activities such as entertaining, family dining, solo relaxation, or even down-and-dirty gardening chores. Or choose lightweight furnishings, keep your plants in wheeled containers, and redesign the scene to suit the occasion.

GO WITH THE FLOW

Some porches and decks are so narrow that any attempt to disguise the fact would be a losing battle. In that case, just accept your structure's limitations as a chance to let your creativity run riot. It matters little whether the style of your container garden is sophisticated, whimsical, or cottage-garden quaint; if the display is eye-catching enough, no one will notice the proportions of the venue.

A purposeful arrangement of containers disguises this deck's narrow, rectangular shape. By themselves, the pots and hanging baskets in the far corners would emphasize the structure's length. But with the addition of a curving border of containers along one wall, the space becomes a well-proportioned dining nook.

Planter boxes, mounted to the outside of the wall, draw the eye upward and outward, thereby visually broadening a deck that's little wider than a ship's passageway.

A simple collection of white tulips blurs the corner and far edge of this deck, leading the eye diagonally across the surface. The result is that the deck doesn't seem narrow at all.

Bench

Fountain

Planters

Planters

FOCUS ON FORM

You may not be able to change the shape of your deck or porch, but a few simple tricks will make it appear more expansive than it really is. L-shaped planter arrangements at both ends lead the eye across the space in a diagonal direction, creating the illusion of a larger area. The bench and fountain, used as focal points, further draw attention away from the deck's short front-to-back dimension.

Personality Plus

The problem: the house you've just purchased comes equipped with a deck that has as much charm as a lump of clay. The solution: use container plants to transform the space from ho-hum to heavenly. You'll be reaching into the same bag of tricks that garden designers use to add visual interest to a dull plot of ground. These styling techniques work just as much magic when the plants are firmly rooted in containers.

BUILD A BORDER

When you want to pack a sophisticated punch, no garden feature beats a lush, flower-filled border. On an in-ground site, that pizzazz can take a lot of time and effort to achieve. On a deck, though, it's a quick cure for the common blahs. Aside from choosing plants and containers that suit your taste and architecture, though, it pays to remember a few other important keys to success.

REPETITION A good design contains elements that repeat. They may be specific plants, or merely color, texture, or shape, or all of the above. And bear in mind that the importance of repetition applies to containers as well as their contents.

SCALE While it is true that plantings look best when they're in keeping with the size of the garden, it's rare that a container plant is too large for its site. It's far more common to err on the side of puniness. When in doubt, think big. A few big containers (the largest size your space can hold) filled with substantial plants will pack a more impressive punch than a jumble of small to midsize pots of fluffy annuals.

STAYING POWER The best borders look good throughout the year. With a border of container plants, you have a couple of options for achieving that goal. You can simply move plants in and out of the spotlight as their moments of glory come and go. Or, your climate permitting, you can assemble combinations of plants that have something to offer season after season— whether flowers, foliage, berries, seedheads, or distinctive branching patterns.

ABOVE LEFT: *Cobalt blue planter boxes of yellow 'Sunburst' coreopsis line up in front of a matching fence.*

LEFT: *The tones of yellow and orange repeat in this potted border, spiked by the icy greenish white colors of 'Envy' zinnias.*

VARY THE TERRAIN

Arranging containers at different heights adds visual punch to any setting, and a banal deck or porch is no exception. Pedestals, baker's racks, and tables allow you to raise the level of a planting scheme without launching a building project. (For more on planting in the vertical dimension, see page 64.) But many decks come already equipped with varied topography—a stairway. Whether tall and steep or low and broad, those wooden treads, and sometimes their handrails, offer a place to display plants on multiple levels.

RIGHT: *Thanks to the owner's collection of weathered metal pots, sap buckets, and watering cans, the stairs of this backdoor porch have personality to spare.*

BELOW: *Terra-cotta pots, filled primarily with herbs and ferns, march up the stairs and across the deck, breaking up a long stretch of board. The containers also fill in the empty space below the railing.*

REFOCUS THE EYE

It's one of the oldest design tricks in the world: when you want to disguise a bland scene (in this case, a boring deck) you simply add new elements that capture attention and refocus the eye. And with plants and containers, the sky's the limit.

Installing a dramatic focal point is an obvious option. A piece of sculpture, a fountain, an outdoor fireplace, or a beautiful furniture grouping will camouflage a less than stellar backdrop. But a successful focal point can be as simple as a corner filled with plants. In fact, it's a symbiotic relationship: flowers and foliage soften the sharp angles of the structure, while the sheltered nook keeps both flora and pots safe from foot traffic.

BELOW: *The pastel tones of striking Asiatic lilies draw all eyes to a corner.*

ABOVE: *Colorful standards never fail to draw attention, especially when they're grouped in eye-catching pots like these white ceramic models. This trio of standards consists of* Solanum, Asclepias, *and pomegranate* (Punica granatum). *Red candles floating in a blue opaline glass bowl add more color to the scene.*

ABOVE: *A pair of sleek chaises and a terra-cotta bowl brimming with succulents turn a plain square of decking into a showplace.*

ABOVE RIGHT: *This grouping refocuses eyes—and fools them, too. The tall pillar candlestick looks like a found architectural fragment, but it's actually a ceramic look-alike. The ceramic containers are masquerading as well-traveled metal boxes.*

RIGHT: *Often the most effective focal points are the simplest. A case in point is this trio of terra-cotta pots filled with ornamental grasses that are different in color but similar in shape and texture.*

Tying It All Together

Aside from enhancing the appearance and usefulness of a porch or deck, container plants perform another important role: linking the structure to the broader landscape, both visually and psychologically.

THE ECHO EFFECT

Whether what lies beyond your porch or deck is your own tiny backyard or a vast stretch of wilderness, there is a simple way to blur the distinction: fill your containers with plants that echo the colors, forms, and textures that appear in the broader arena. That doesn't mean duplicating the varieties of plants themselves. In fact, this trick works even if there are no plants to be seen. For instance, if your deck overlooks a broad body of water and you want your view to flow seamlessly, choose fine-textured foliage in the gray-blue range and flower colors in soft, watery tones of mauve, blue, lavender, and white.

BY CONTRAST

But what if you want to make the viewer's eye leap across the boundary of your deck and into the distant scenery? In that case, at the farthest edge of your structure, place a container planting that contrasts sharply in color and texture with the landscape beyond.

FAR LEFT: *A container of soft pinks and grays blurs the border between the deck and the lawn, leading the eye into the broader picture.*

LEFT: *Staged for a garden show, this setting carries the tying-together concept to the level of an art form. Stainless steel containers on the deck mimic the walls of raised beds and even pathway risers in the garden beyond. Likewise, the colors and rounded shapes of the plants remain consistent throughout the scene.*

ABOVE: *In a garden filled with rich green foliage and clouds of white tulips, it's all but impossible to tell where the container-filled deck ends and the rest of the garden begins.*

LEFT: *Plantings, in containers or otherwise, don't come more dramatic than these floral "bonfires" marking the edge of a deck that's also a dock. At sunset, the flowers cast their own red glow on the water, blending with the tones from the sky.*

Save That Surface

Container gardening is certainly not a hazardous pastime, but it can be risky for your bank account if your garden sits atop a wooden deck or porch. Even pressure-treated and rot-resistant woods will deteriorate under the steady onslaught of water runoff and fertilizer salts. Tile and masonry surfaces are more durable, but even they can suffer from the by-products of plant care. Although the damage may take a long time to materialize, water and fertilizers can create ugly stains on pricey hardscape. Some protective measures are in order.

PAINT ON PROTECTION

It's crucial to coat all wooden surfaces with a high-quality, water-repellent sealer every two or three years. Adding exterior stain or paint over the sealer will give you longer-term protection. Commercial coatings are available to protect brick, tile, and concrete—and to remove stains that are already in place. A couple of other simple measures can help, too.

CATCH THE DRIPS Either use nonporous saucers or set draining pots inside other containers without holes. To waterproof untreated terra-cotta, simply paint the interior with clear acrylic enamel. Besides ending drips, you'll also cut back on water lost to evaporation through the container's sides.

DIRECT THE DRIPS Whenever possible, position hanging baskets and window boxes so that they drain onto open ground, not onto the porch or deck surface.

LEFT: *Wheeled plant trolleys catch water before it drips to the decking below. They also make it easy to push plants to shelter when cold—or steamy—weather spells trouble.*

FACING PAGE, BOTTOM: *The ultimate in deck protection: a built-in, bottomless planter that drains directly to the soil. If your deck doesn't have one of these designs, you can achieve the same effect by constructing planters on the ground along the structure's edges.*

RIGHT: *Stainless steel trays, tailor-made to fit their painted wooden containers, keep drips from touching this deck's surface. In the boxes: hostas, ferns, and bamboo.*

BELOW: *These railing-mounted planters of scarlet geraniums drain mostly on the deck; if the planters were mounted outside the railing, they would drain directly on the ground.*

Havens for Butterflies and Hummingbirds

Even the smallest container garden can offer a warm welcome for these jewels on the wing. Your best floral choices for attracting nectar-sippers depend on your area of the country, but you'll find good starter lists of plants on these pages.

Plants to Lure Butterflies

The sipping tastes of butterflies are more wide-ranging than those of hummingbirds. Their favorites, though, are daisy-type blooms and any plant with small flowers arranged in clusters or spikes. Butterflies love all colors, but purple tops the list.

Blanket flower, annual *(Gaillardia pulchella)*
Butterfly weed *(Asclepias tuberosa)*
Common heliotrope *(Heliotropium arborescens)*
Cosmos
Dahlia
Four o'clock *(Mirabilis jalapa)*
Mexican sunflower *(Tithonia rotundifolia)*
Pink *(Dianthus)*
Sweet alyssum *(Lobularia maritima)*

RIGHT: *A trio of pots provides food for butterfly larvae and nectar for adults. The pot on the left features purple Mexican bush sage* (Salvia leucantha), *pale yellow lantana,* Coreopsis verticillata *'Zagreb', and pale purple aster. The front pot combines purple heliotrope, 'Early Sunrise' coreopsis, and yellow lantana. The tallest pot contains orange lion's tail* (Leonotis leonurus), *blood flower* (Asclepias curassavica), *and pale yellow lantana. The shallow stone bowl holds water for both butterflies and larvae.*

Plants to Lure Hummingbirds

Hummingbirds favor flowers that are tubular in shape, with blossoms arranged around stems so that tubes point outward, and without leaves or branches to get in the way of their whirring wings. Red and orange colors draw these tiny birds like magnets; however, they are also fond of blue flowers.

Canna
Coral bells *(Heuchera)*
Cypress vine *(Ipomoea quamoclit)*
Daylily *(Hemerocallis)*
Fuchsia
Lily *(Lilium)*
Lobelia *(Lobelia erinus)*
Parrot's beak *(Lotus berthelotii)*
Petunia × hybrida
Sage *(Salvia)*

ABOVE: *Although red and reddish orange blooms are famed as hummingbird drawing cards, the tiny wingers are also fond of blue flowers like these 'Heavenly Blue' morning glories. Their appeal lies in the tubular-shaped blossoms, which stand out from the foliage, thereby allowing the birds' wings to flap unimpeded as their beaks probe deeply for nectar.*

Old-Fashioned Charmer

All across the country, old-time porches are staging a big-time comeback. For many home owners, the reason is aesthetic: some types of houses simply look better with porches. Others want to recapture the spirit of a time when everyone gathered on porches, lemonade in hand, to visit with neighbors, greet passersby, and watch children play. Regardless of the purpose a porch serves in your life, it is the perfect setting for simple, old-fashioned flowers.

BEFORE

A wicker loveseat nestles between pots while cushions of flowers soften the porch's straight-edged design. Among the blooms are Oriental lilies (Lilium), *white 'Palace' miniature roses, white marguerites, yellow strawflowers* (Bracteantha bracteata), *and a pink hydrangea.*

A caladium (Caladium bicolor) *and an ornamental asparagus fern* (Asparagus densiflorus) *form a billowy mound in the corner. Pink miniature roses punch up the foreground.*

COME SIT A SPELL

What do you do when your beautiful old house sports a porch that complements its architecture perfectly—but the space is a bare, uninviting rectangle? The answer is easy: just gather up some attractive pots and fill them with simple old-time plants. Add comfortable wicker furniture, and you've got the perfect spot to put up your feet and shift your mind into low gear.

FACING PAGE, BOTTOM: *At the far end of the porch, geraniums climb up bamboo supports. Pink hydrangeas flank the front door, and pink and white petunias tumble from boxes on the porch railing. Terra-cotta pots spill over with lilies, daisies, and miniature roses by the dozens.*

Longtime Favorites

All of these simple annuals and tender perennials (usually treated as annuals) perform well in containers and look perfectly at home on a classic porch. What's more, many of them are deliciously fragrant.

American marigold (Tagetes erecta)
Baby's breath (Gypsophila paniculata)
Bachelor's button (Centaurea cyanus)
Common heliotrope (Heliotropium arborescens)
Cosmos
Dame's rocket (Hesperis matronalis)
Evening scented stock (Matthiola longipetala bicornis)
Flowering tobacco (Nicotiana alata and N. sylvestris for flowers and fragrance)
Four o'clock (Mirabilis jalapa)
Garden nasturtium (Tropaeolum majus)
Love-in-a-mist (Nigella damascena)
Mignonette (Reseda odorata)
Morning glory (Ipomoea tricolor)
Pincushion flower (Scabiosa caucasica)
Primrose (Primula)
Snapdragon (Antirrhinum majus)
Stock (Matthiola incana)
Sweet alyssum (Lobularia maritima)
Sweet pea (Lathyrus odoratus)

CHAPTER FOUR

Patios, Courtyards, and Terraces

IN THE PAST DECADE OR SO, people all across the country have discovered what dwellers in balmy climates have always known—that patios (and their alter egos, courtyards and terraces) can function as real outdoor rooms, not simply places to park a barbecue grill. The interest in container gardening has risen hand in hand with the popularity of open-air living. After all, well-chosen plants in attractive pots not only decorate outdoor spaces, but they can also divide them, letting you carve out separate nooks for entertaining, family dining, solo lounging, or even working with your laptop computer. Furthermore, if you choose your living "room dividers" with portability in mind, you can easily move them from place to place to suit the activity of the day or the weather of the season.

A padded bench and attractive container plantings turn a courtyard into a lush garden hideaway.

Possibilities Aplenty

How do you design a container garden that will turn your paved piece of real estate into outdoor living quarters? Start by studying the photographs on the following pages. As you peruse these photos, note what colors, textures, and styles appeal to you in plants, pots, and accessories. If you are drawn to a garden filled with plants that would never work in your climate, remember that you can achieve the same feeling with plants better suited to your area.

ABOVE LEFT: *Huge terra-cotta pots filled with greenery set the tone on this elegant wraparound terrace.*

LEFT: *Boxwood balls in tall pots mark the entrance to an urban patio. Italian limestone paves the floor and tops the table.*

ABOVE: *In Mexico and Spain, gardeners brighten court-yards by filling them with colorful annuals in a multitude of pots. In this adobe-walled retreat in Phoenix, petunias reign in vibrant shades of red and pink, accented by splashes of purple and white.*

RIGHT: *A water garden surrounded by containers of foliage plants forms the centerpiece of this venerable, tranquil courtyard.*

RIGHT: *Standards like these "lolli-pop" bays add a formal touch to any garden. The braided trunks are actually the result of training two shoots around a supporting stake. Growing a bay "tree" this size takes several years, so if you want formality fast, buy fin-ished models at the nursery. (For more on standards, see page 113.)*

BELOW: *Wisteria-covered walls, pots spilling over with white petunias, and subdued lighting beckon evening swimmers to this lap pool. (For more on gardens that shine after dark, see pages 68–69.)*

FACING PAGE, TOP: *Jolts of cobalt blue make a strong statement on this terrace carved out of a hillside. Plants include hostas, cannas, and phormiums. A palm in a huge urn takes center stage, while blue ceramic wedges surrounding the pot provide extra seating.*

FACING PAGE, BOTTOM LEFT: *Pots of violas add spots of color to a neutral-toned patio that functions as an outdoor living room.*

FACING PAGE, BOTTOM RIGHT: *It took relatively few plants to turn a small, bare space into a verdant niche. This size of this tiny courtyard also allowed the owner to splurge on intricate stone paving.*

FACING PAGE, TOP LEFT: *Striking pots, ornamental grasses, and succulents give this high-walled courtyard an architectural feel.*

FACING PAGE, TOP RIGHT: *For a courtyard garden that's used mostly at night, the owners chose white walls and raised beds, clipped boxwood, and standard photinias. Uplights and candles on the planter edges supply even more drama.*

FACING PAGE, BOTTOM: *Cool blue flowers and rich greenery underscore the billowy forms and earthy hues of ornamental grasses. Featured here are fountain grass (*Pennisetum setaceum *'Rubrum'), Sinaloa sage (*Salvia sinaloensis), *and Japanese silver grass (*Miscanthus sinensis *'Yaku Jima').*

ABOVE: *Completely surrounded by high building walls, this courtyard has what nearly every urbanite craves—privacy and quiet. Thanks to painted lattice and a light-colored stone floor, enough light reaches the scene to please the calla lilies and the houseplants spending their summer outdoors.*

LEFT: *With distinctive patterns on house walls and terrace floors, this container garden benefits from a simple color palette. Purple flowers accent the green and white scene supplied by foliage plants and calla lilies.*

Living in the Light

Like all garden sites, patios have their challenges. Two of the biggest can be either too little or too much sun. A cool, shady courtyard is a treat for people, but it limits choices for container plants. At the other extreme, an enclosed patio can trap and hold the sun's rays. Without deep layers of cool soil to protect their roots, container plants are especially vulnerable to blistering heat. Fortunately, you have some excellent coping mechanisms at your disposal for either situation.

TOO MUCH OF A GOOD THING

Depending on where you live, you might have as much trouble grasping the concept of "too much sunlight" as a five-year-old would have imagining a birthday party with "too many toys." But for container gardeners in many parts of the country, sheltering plants from the sun's harsh rays can be a major undertaking. If your patio has less protection from the sun than you would like, call on the following strategies for help.

MAKE INSTANT SHADE Place free-standing screens or panels of lath or canvas where they'll block the most intense sunlight. You can construct your own or purchase ready-made protectors that are either permanent or retractable, in styles ranging from rustic to elegant.

GROW SHADE Position containers holding rough and rugged trees, shrubs, or vines where they will cast shade on more sensitive plants. The best choices will depend on your particular situation, but it's wise to look for plants native to your region that prefer full, intense sun.

BELOW: *Potted climbing roses thrive in full sun on the outside pillars of a pergola. But under its roof, people can dine in shady comfort.*

Glass windows intensify the light and heat that reach this patio. Dahlias cheerfully soak up the sun, while a fence and umbrella shield the owners from its rays.

PLAY AROUND

When you're shopping for container plants, don't simply take the sun/shade recommendations in books and catalogs at face value. A plant that prefers full sun in one region may thrive in far lower light someplace else. For instance, in northern latitudes the long hours of daylight in the summer can compensate for a lack of direct sunshine. And in the South and Southwest, or at high altitudes anywhere, even the most sun-loving plants benefit from some midday shade. So how do you know what to put where? Experiment. (Remember that transportability is one of the great beauties of container gardening!) Move your plants around until you find the light level that suits them best, and give them shelter when needed.

MIND THE BACKGROUND Keep container plants away from sources of reflected light. Mirrors, glass doors, windows, and light-colored masonry walls reflect and intensify both sunlight and heat. At best, these conditions will give your plants a thirst that won't quit; at worst, they will cook your plants' roots.

AVOID BLACK CONTAINERS Whether hand-thrown ceramic creations or plastic nursery pots, black containers capture and retain heat. That can be a real plus in a cool climate, but in a warm climate with hot temperatures it can spell disaster for your container plants.

KEEP THEM MOVING An advantage of container gardening is that you can move pots around to suit changing light levels. If your site demands a periodic game of hide-and-seek with the sun, keep sensitive plants on wheeled dollies or grouped on a decorative cart. You need only roll them from sun to shade or vice versa.

RIGHT: *Lady's-mantle* (Alchemilla), *lamb's ears* (Stachys byzantina), *and bacopa* (Sutera cordata) *bask in the light shade under trees.*

In a hot climate or at high altitudes, sunlight is more intense. Translation: these cannas, nasturtiums (Tropaeolum), and blank flowers (Gaillardia × grandiflora), and other plants commonly described as needing full sun, can thrive on less.

MORE LIGHT, PLEASE

You may not be able to increase the amount of sun that reaches your site, but there are ways you can increase the potency of the light you have. For instance, mirrors hung on or propped against walls or fences will catch and magnify any light that reaches them. Water performs the same feat. A small fountain, a potted water garden, or even a birdbath will make your garden lighter. Likewise, white or very pale walls and floor surfaces reflect light onto nearby plants—and make your garden appear more spacious at the same time.

58

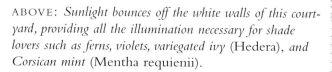

ABOVE: *Sunlight bounces off the white walls of this court-yard, providing all the illumination necessary for shade lovers such as ferns, violets, variegated ivy* (Hedera), *and Corsican mint* (Mentha requienii).

FACING PAGE, BOTTOM: *Even heavily shaded gardens like this one can be delightfully lush, as long as you're happy with plenty of foliage and few flowers. Ivies in par-ticular perform well in low-light settings; even plants that prefer some sun will flourish but may bloom sparsely.*

ABOVE: *Here's a textbook example of improving the hand you've been dealt. The designers of this passage have pulled out all the stops to increase the light level, including painting the walls white and installing a white-tiled floor and borders around the planting beds.*

Shades of Difference

Shade is not an absolute like the numbers on a thermometer. In gardening terms, light—or the lack thereof—is broken down into six basic categories:

■ FULL SUN means 6 or more hours of direct sunlight a day. This is what most vegetables need to perform their best.

■ PART SUN or PART SHADE means that the site receives anywhere from 2 to 5 hours of sun a day. The effect of sun-light on plants depends not only on how long it lasts but also on how intense it is, and that varies enormously depending on time of day, time of year, and even altitude and latitude. (See "Play Around" on page 57.)

■ FILTERED LIGHT comes through the small leaves of trees like willows or birches, the openings in a trellis or arbor, or a translucent canopy. When a book or catalog says a plant performs well in shade, more often than not it really means filtered light. Many excellent container plants fall into this category, including hosta, astilbe, and dead nettle *(Lamium)*.

■ DAPPLED SHADE is cast by large-leafed trees, like oaks, maples, and hickories. Though foliage blocks the sun, light still comes through. Impatiens, early-blooming bulbs, and vio-las perform well in dappled shade.

■ BRIGHT LIGHT is a common condition in city gardens and other densely built areas. It means that no direct sun reaches the site but nothing blocks the sky. Azaleas, rhodo-dendrons, and camellias do beautifully in bright light.

■ DENSE SHADE is cast by tall, north-facing walls or the low, dense branches of evergreen trees. Many ivies thrive in dense shade, but few flowering plants can survive for long.

A Design Primer

Even when a patio lacks enclosing walls, it can easily function as an outdoor room. And no matter the style of your decor—from cutting-edge trendy to down-home country—designing with portable plantings can help create exactly the mood and look you want.

TRICKS OF THE TRADE

You don't have to be a design professional to turn an empty patio into your favorite spot to entertain or relax. With a few plants in pots and the simple design ideas on the following pages, you can create a movable garden that transforms your space, from serene to dramatic and from cozy to grand.

KEEP IT SIMPLE A garden with a palette of one or two colors (especially white or pastels) plus green, in similar or identical containers, looks more spacious than one with a crazy-quilt mixture of shades in a jumble of pots.

Perfectly trimmed boxwood balls marching up a set of stairs lend an air of sleek uniformity to this scene.

To make a small space seem bigger, opt for a limited color palette like the green and pink color scheme on this patio.

Don't confuse "just green" with "simple." Here, a bronzey Cordyline fans out above golden 'Garden Party' and 'So Dainty' dahlias.

The brilliant reds of cannas, dahlias, and Crocosmia dance against a blue-framed window.

ABOVE: *An orange wall is a dramatic backdrop for a simple but striking quartet of white lilies.*

DO IT WITH MIRRORS Besides increasing the light level in a garden, mirrors hung in strategic places deceive the eye, creating an illusion of space and multiplying the plantings. Just make sure you place the mirrors where they won't reflect the viewer, thereby giving the game away.

USE PERSPECTIVE As we all learned in grade-school art class, distant objects appear smaller than those close at hand. One simple way to make this principle work in your garden is to find two potted plants that are identical in everything but size. (Boxwood balls or ivy on topiary frames would be perfect.) Set the larger one in the foreground and the smaller one at the far-thest point possible. Your eye will perceive the small plant—and therefore your boundary—as being farther away than it really is. If your garden has room for several sizes of plants, that's even better.

DON'T CROWD Do use distinctive containers to highlight entry points, play up architectural fea-tures, and delineate walkways. But leave plenty of room for people and pets to move around in comfort. How much space you need depends on how you use the area. For instance, the rule of thumb for dining is to allow 3 feet on all sides of the table when the chairs are pulled back. (If you can only dream about having that much room, just do the best you can!)

TOP: *With just two big pots, this small pool patio has ample room for swimmers to move about in comfort.*

ABOVE: *In this restrained garden, tall, trim planters line the walkway; one marks the entrance to a tiny dining area—leaving plenty of room for a bistro table and chairs.*

SPOTLIGHT A SUBJECT The world is full of beautiful plants, pots, and garden accessories. But too many of them in one place add up to clutter. To make a tiny garden look and "live" bigger, opt for a few choice plants in simple pots and one dramatic focal point. A fountain or a sculpture will do the trick. So will a found treasure, such as a big, quirky piece of driftwood or a massive boulder.

ABOVE: *If you have limited space and a limited container budget, focus on a fabulous find. One-of-a-kind planters are worthy of a splurge.*

TOP RIGHT: *A sundial is a classic attention-getter, especially when it's surrounded by billows of potted geraniums. Two standards in pots flank the garden gate.*

RIGHT: *Nothing adds drama like a fountain—even one without water. Here, a cascade of white bacopa gushes forth. Under the cherub's toes is a froth of bell-flowers (Campanula) and strawberries.*

The Vertical Dimension

Like other prime container-gardening venues, patios are often less than capacious. Whether your quarters are tight or you always seem to need room for just one more pot (well, maybe two), these tricks will help you make the most of every inch of growing space.

ABOVE: *Terra-cotta pots, both natural and painted blue, adorn a patio wall in Cordoba, Spain.*

FROM THE GROUND UP Vines grown in containers will scramble up trellises and posts as lustily as their in-ground relatives. What's more, rampant growers and self-seeders such as morning glory, anemone clematis *(C. montana),* and some honeysuckles are easier to keep within bounds when their roots are in pots.

HANG IT Wall-mounted planters and baskets cloak walls and fences in greenery and free up valuable floor space at the same time. Stick with one style for a more sophisticated look, or go all out with a mixture of designs and materials.

ABOVE: *An urban gardener has taken full advantage of every planting space in this tiny courtyard.*

RIGHT: *In a no-soil situation, big pots of scarlet cypress vine* (Ipomoea quamoclit) *bring vibrant color to a narrow patio.*

STACK THEM Baker's racks, étagères, and even stepladders give you vertical planting space without the need for additional wall attachments.

Trellises and hanging baskets aren't the only means of adding vertical planting space. A simple stepladder can hold multiple pots—with no hardware needed.

LEFT: *Built-in risers lift this herb garden out of the ordinary.*

RIGHT: *Flames of orange lantana leap from a retired fire bucket; icy gray leaves of licorice plant (Helichrysum petiolare) lower the heat.*

A savvy use of repetition—in this case of both color and plants—makes this gray, stone terrace a winner. Red geraniums in pots and planting beds are echoed in the window box and hanging baskets.

A simple baker's rack can increase planting space by many times its small footprint. In this garden, there's room for a bird-house and the owner's collection of culinary herbs and edible flowers, including sage, thyme, rosemary, and nasturtiums.

Espalier

Espalier, the art of training a tree or shrub to grow more or less flat against a wall or fence, is a classic space-saver. It's also a surprisingly simple way to add a touch of sophistication to any container garden. Potted, dwarf fruit trees make excellent candidates for formal shaping. Simply fasten a trellis or wires to a fence or wall and set the tree in its pot 8 to 12 inches away. As the tree grows, prune off any branches that stick out, and tie those remaining to the trellis or wires to form either a series of horizontal branches or a fan pattern. (Apple and pear trees take well to horizontal espaliers; cherries are most often fan-trained.)

For a more free-form espalier, set a potted tree or shrub in front of a wall, fence, or trellis and allow it to branch naturally. As the plant grows, clip off anything that juts out. The key to success is consistency: check the plant every few weeks during the growing season.

1 Choose two strong branches to form the first tier; remove all other shoots and cut back the leader (the main trunk) to just above the bottom wire. Bend the branches at a 45-degree angle and secure them to the wire with soft cloth or plastic ties.

2 During the first growing season, gradually tighten the ties so that by the end of the season the branches are horizontal. When the newly sprouted leader is long enough, hold it erect and tie it to the second wire.

3 During the first dormant season, cut back the leader to the second wire. Choose two branches for the second tier and remove competing shoots. Cut lateral growth on the lower branches back to three buds.

4 During the second growing season, gradually bring the second-tier branches to a horizontal position, as described above in step 2. Keep the leader upright and tie it to the third wire.

5 Repeat the process for a fourth wire, if desired. When the leader reaches the top wire, cut it back to just above the top branch. Keep horizontal branches in bounds by pruning back the ends to downward-facing side branches in late spring and summer.

Creating an informal espalier is a simpler process. As the tree or shrub grows, clip off shoots that jut out too far from the wall or fence. Plants with a naturally horizontal branching pattern, such as cotoneaster (depicted above), work well for informal training.

Some Enchanted Evenings

If you're like many busy people, chances are you seldom even see your garden during the daylight hours, much less have a chance to relax and enjoy it. So why not design a container garden that comes into its own at dusk—just when you're free to settle in and soak up its charms?

BEFORE

White pots and flowers alike glow in candlelight. The large container holds calla lilies (Zantedeschia) *and Clematis 'Garland'. To the right, an autumn fern* (Dryopteris erythrosora) *cloaks the "feet" of a moth orchid* (Phalaenopsis). *An azalea spills over the pot in the foreground.*

The white-margined leaves of Hosta fortunei *'Green Gold' take center stage here. In the pots surrounding them are (clockwise from top right) moth orchids, an autumn fern, New Guinea impatiens 'Pearl White', and pansy orchids* (Miltoniopsis).

INTO THE NIGHT

This covered patio had all the makings of a charming outdoor sitting room, but no one ever used it. Now it's become the family's favorite after-work gathering spot. The key to a garden that beckons at night can be summed up in one word: white. Plants with white flowers or white-margined leaves hold their own at dusk and beyond, long after even pastel tones have vanished into the darkness.

FACING PAGE, BOTTOM: *White flowers, white pots, and glowing candles set the stage for relaxing evenings in this container garden.*

Plants for an Evening Garden

The plants listed here are annuals and tender perennials that are grown as annuals in most parts of the country.

Aster (any dwarf white variety)

Baby's breath *(Gypsophila paniculata)*

Common sunflower *(Helianthus annuus* **'Italian White')**

Cosmos *(Cosmos bipinnatus* **'Sonata White')**

Evergreen candytuft *(Iberis sempervirens)*

Flowering tobacco *(Nicotiana alata* **or** *N. sylvestris* **for evening fragrance; not the Nicki** or Domino strains often sold at garden centers)

Four o'clock *(Mirabilis jalapa)*

Gardenia *(Gardenia augusta)*

***Impatiens* (any white variety; the Fiesta series has an attractive double type)**

Iris (any white variety)

Love-in-a-mist *(Nigella damascena* **'Miss Jekyll Alba')**

Moonflower *(Ipomoea alba)*

Poet's jasmine *(Jasminum officinale)*

Snow-in-summer *(Cerastium tomentosum)*

Spider flower *(Cleome hasslerana* **'Helen Campbell')**

Tuberose *(Polianthes tuberosa)*

Tuberous begonia (any white variety)

Tulip *(Tulipa,* **any white variety)**

CHAPTER FIVE

Roof Gardens and Balconies

ANY GARDEN CAN BE a place of beauty and repose, but a garden perched on a balcony or a rooftop is more than that. For many city dwellers, and for increasing numbers of suburbanites, it's a cherished, private slice of the great outdoors. Whether it's a sprawling rooftop oasis or a balcony scarcely big enough to stand on, a garden-on-high is like a verdant magic carpet, soaring above a world of noise and hard-edged technology. ❧ That's the human viewpoint. From a plant's perspective, that elevated Eden is hostile territory. Because sun and wind become more intense as distance from the ground increases, both top growth and potted roots are far more vulnerable to weather than they are at ground level. Without proper protection, even the hardiest vegetation can suffer. The good news is that by choosing your plants carefully and taking some simple precautions, you can enjoy a beautiful and thriving green scene, even high above terra firma.

A verdant roof garden seems light-years away from the busy street below.

Coping with the Elements

On a small, shady balcony that normally gets only light, balmy breezes, your plants may need no added protection at all. But be prepared to cover them or whisk them indoors if the weather turns blustery. On a wide-open rooftop, both plants and people benefit from structures that filter sun and block wind. And if you live where strong gusts are commonplace, you'll probably want to construct built-in planters or anchor containers to the floor or walls.

LEFT: *Vine-covered trellises and adjoining buildings shield this rooftop sitting area from wind and harsh sun.*

ABOVE: *It may be wide open to the big-city sky, but with its sheltering walls and comfortable furniture, this penthouse garden has all the charm of a country living room.*

RIGHT: *This elevated garden features tempered glass panels to block wind, a heavy and all-but-indestructible railway sleeper bench, and firmly anchored planters. Inside the planters are* Phormium tenax *'Rainbow Queen' and P. 'Platts Black'—rugged New Zealand natives that can take all the sun and wind that come their way.*

HOLD IT RIGHT THERE!

On a rooftop or high balcony, strong winds can topple both plants and furniture or even send them sailing—sometimes with disastrous results. When you garden in the air, you'll need to consider some factors aside from design and horticulture.

WEIGHTY MATTERS While it is true that lightweight pots filled with ultralight planting mix will put the least strain on structural supports, they're also easy to knock over, especially when they hold large plants. The same weight considerations apply to furniture and decorative objects. Anything made of plastic, tubular metal, or lightweight wood is too flimsy to stay in place for long. You may need to experiment to find containers and furnishings that strike the ideal balance between too heavy and too light.

ABOVE: *These wooden planters with attached, camellia-covered trellises soften the walls much more effectively than a collection of pots could. What's more, the structures are sturdy enough to stay firmly rooted in place through all but the fiercest gales.*

LEFT: *Built-in wooden planters keep pots of herbs securely in place on this tiny riverfront balcony.*

TIES THAT BIND At truly lofty heights or in extremely windy areas, it pays to anchor even heavy containers and furnishings (including barbecue grills) to floors or walls. Better yet, opt for built-in planters and furniture.

WORST-CASE SCENARIO Ask your insurance agent whether your home-owner's or renter's policy covers damage inflicted by objects falling from your balcony or roof. If the answer is no, it might be wise to add coverage.

A low railing with tempered-glass inserts provides all the protection this Washington, D.C., roof garden needs and leaves a clear view of the Potomac meandering below. Ceramic pots and a lightweight metal table and chaises are easily stored for the winter.

HOLD IT DOWN

On a rooftop, high balcony, or other exposed location, it's wise to anchor trees and tall shrubs so that they won't topple and break in gusty winds. It's a simple task in a wooden planter. Screw sturdy eye-hooks into the sides of the container (one anchor per major limb). Then run support wire from the limbs to the hooks. Use adjustable hardware so that you can lengthen the lines as the tree grows. Prevent damage to the bark by wrapping the wire in rubber or plastic tubing. If your trees are growing in stone or concrete planters, use screw-in hooks designed for masonry.

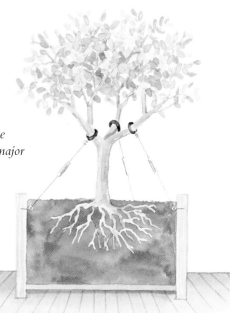

Standing Fast

While any plant can fall victim to strong gusts, the following trees and shrubs tolerate more wind than most.

Bayberry (Myrica pensylvanica)
Birch (Betula)
Cinquefoil (Potentilla)
Common privet (Ligustrum vulgare)
Cotoneaster
Flowering crabapple (Malus)
Juniper (Juniperus)
Pussy willow (Salix discolor)
Russian olive (Elaeagnus angustifolia)
Yew (Taxus)

Weight and Drainage

Even more than weather, two factors are crucial to the success of a rooftop or balcony garden: safe weight distribution and efficient water drainage.

WEIGHT

How elaborate your weight investigation must be depends on the size of your intended garden and the type, age, and condition of your building.

If you live in a recently built house, condominium, or apartment building, the contractor, home-owners' association, or landlord should be able to advise you about safe weight limits, as

ABOVE: *The owners of this roof terrace came up with a clever drainage plan: a gravel border extending around the perimeter of the floor. Large containers are strategically positioned over structural beams.*

LEFT: *Symmetry serves a double purpose in this elegant roof garden. The corner placement of cotoneaster and boxwood topiaries in stone containers lends a formal air to the urban sanctuary and, more important, spreads the weight around. With the heavy planters resting on secure supports, the decking can easily handle the hefty load of the cast-iron furniture.*

well as any design restrictions or local building codes.

In the case of an older structure—or if your plans call for anything more elaborate than a few lightweight pots—get a structural survey. For a modest sum, a structural engineer can tell you the weight tolerances of every part of your roof or balcony, as well as the condition of any walls, fences, and railings. If possible, get a personal recommendation from an architect or builder whose judgment you trust; failing that, look under "Engineers—Structural" in the yellow pages. Use a licensed engineer and make sure you are provided with a detailed written report. Avoid low-cost "semi-pros" who employ such tactics as jumping up and down on a roof to test its strength.

HOW HEAVY IS IT?

The load-bearing capacity of your structure will affect your choices of floors, containers, and furnishings. Here are the weights of common building and garden materials.

MATERIAL	POUNDS PER CUBIC FOOT	KILOGRAMS PER CUBIC METER
Brickwork (average)	115	1,865
Cast iron	450	7,297
Concrete: Lightweight	80–100	1,298–1,622
Precast	130	2,108
Reinforced	150	2,433
Granite	170	2,757
Gravel	120	1,946
Limestone	155	2,514
Marble	170	2,757
Pebbles	120	1,946
Sandstone	145	2,352
Slate	160–180	2,595–2,919
Tile and setting bed	15–73 lbs./sq. ft.	73–353 kg/sq. m
Timber: Hardwood (average)	45	730
Softwood (average)	35	568
Water	62.428	1,013

Source: Reprinted by permission of The McGraw-Hill Companies, from Charles W. Harris and Nicholas Dines, eds., *Time Saver Standards for Landscape Architecture,* 2nd edition (New York: McGraw-Hill, 1997).

LIGHTEN THE LOAD

Attractive, high-tech container materials and ultralight potting mixes give aboveground gardeners many options for reducing weight without having to sacrifice aesthetics.

The simplest way to lighten the load on your building is to fill your planters with a commercial seed-germinating mix, which weighs less than regular potting soils. If you use self-watering pots, a seed starter has another advantage over more conventional mixes—its coarse texture allows moisture to rise much more readily from the reservoir on the bottom. One note of caution: Because a seed starter contains no nutrients, you'll need to be very diligent

A layer of overturned plastic nursery pots and foam peanuts can make heavy containers suitable for use on roof gardens and balconies.

about fertilizing. Use a slow-release granular fertilizer at the recommended rate; it should last about four months.

Lightweight Potting Mix

If you prefer to make your own lightweight soil, here's a simple recipe:

- 5 gallons of ground sphagnum moss or coir fiber
- 5 gallons of vermiculite or perlite
- 2 gallons of compost
- 1 cup of granular, slow-release fertilizer

The end product weighs about the same as a seed-starting mix and has two sizable advantages: The compost supplies trace nutrients and, according to recent evidence, inhibits the growth of disease-causing fungi and bacteria. The scoop holds a mix of compost, perlite, sphagnum moss, and slow-release fertilizer (clockwise from top).

REDUCE THE VOLUME

Very large containers are heavy even when they're filled with lightweight mixes. To reduce both weight and the amount of planting mix you'll have to buy, fill the pot about one-third to one-half with light, bulky material, such as beer or soda cans, plastic pots, or chunks of plastic foam, before you add soil. (If you use packing "peanuts," make sure they're not made from corn-starch, which will soon dissolve.) This technique works well for annuals and shallow-rooted perennials grown in large pots, but don't use it for trees or shrubs, which need all the root room they can get.

DRAINAGE

Even if your garden consists of only a few featherweight containers, you need to know one crucial piece of information: where the water goes when it leaves the pots. The same engineer who determines your structure's load-bearing capacity can investigate your roof and walls for potential leaks. If there are flaws, no matter how minor, have them attended to before you lay down any flooring or arrange your plants. Make sure the floor surface (new or existing) slopes gently toward drains. Keep container weight as light as possible, given wind conditions, and use platforms or decks to distribute heavy loads over a broader area.

AN OUNCE OF PREVENTION To prevent drainage trouble in the future, keep a watchful eye out. In particular:

- Keep drains and downspouts free of debris and unobstructed by containers, furniture, or flooring materials.
- Check your plants' roots periodically, and when you find them poking through drainage holes, trim them back or move the plants to bigger quarters. Otherwise, they could grow into floor joints or wall crevices in search of water.

UP AND AWAY
Water and fertilizer salts can spell trouble for both floor surfaces and roof structures. To avoid stains and leaks, keep saucers under pots and arrange containers, furniture, and accessories so that all drains remain clear.

Flooring Choices

In large part, your garden-surface options depend on the weight-bearing capacity of your roof or balcony (see page 76). The strongest roofs can handle the same kinds of paving you might use in a conventional garden. You can even spread soil and plant a lawn, if you want to.

OPTIONS UNDERFOOT

There are other factors to consider, though, including climate, budget, whether you own or rent your home, and how long you intend to be there. For example, if you live in a rental apartment and plan to move in a year or two, you may want to install a floor you can pick up and take with you. The style of your garden, as well as its purpose, will also influence your choices. Will you use it as an outdoor living area or simply as display space for plants?

Varied as they are, flooring materials break down into three basic categories:

PAVING On the upside, paving sets a tone of sophistication and permanence. With a virtually limitless range of tiles, bricks, concrete slabs, and natural stone to choose from, it's easy to find one that suits your taste, style, and budget.

On the downside, paving is heavy, some materials are affected by freezing temperatures, and aboveground installation requires extra care to allow for drainage. You can either set pavers on battens or pads to lift them clear of the roof, or spread a layer of free-draining gravel over the roof and set tiles into it, leaving the joints open.

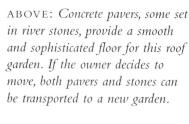

ABOVE: *Concrete pavers, some set in river stones, provide a smooth and sophisticated floor for this roof garden. If the owner decides to move, both pavers and stones can be transported to a new garden.*

LEFT: *Quarry tile makes a fine floor in a mild climate like that of London, the home of this thriving roof garden.*

FACING PAGE, BOTTOM LEFT: *Gravel provides excellent drainage for a roof garden; slate tiles make for easier walking and plant tending.*

GRAVEL AND STONE CHIPS They are inexpensive, easy to install, and available in a range of colors and sizes. Their uneven surface makes them less than ideal for sitting and dining areas, but you can set stepping-stones into them to make walking easier.

DECKING It has some distinct advantages over other materials. For one thing, you can easily suspend it above the roof surface, which allows for free drainage. Installation can be permanent or temporary, and you can make or buy modular sections that are simple to lift for maintenance— or for loading into a moving van. Traditional wood decking requires periodic cleaning and sealing, but new versions made from composite lumber or recycled plastic lumber need no upkeep beyond an occasional hosing. What's more, these new lumbers are slip-resistant when wet and splinter-free.

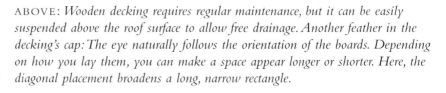

ABOVE: *Wooden decking requires regular maintenance, but it can be easily suspended above the roof surface to allow free drainage. Another feather in the decking's cap: The eye naturally follows the orientation of the boards. Depending on how you lay them, you can make a space appear longer or shorter. Here, the diagonal placement broadens a long, narrow rectangle.*

Safe and Sound

Protective railings are a crucial part of any balcony or roof garden. Not only do they keep people, pets, and plants from going overboard, but they can also block unpleasant views or play up good ones, help muffle noise, and provide vertical planting space.

ABOVE LEFT: *An open-mesh steel and wire railing, a bistro table and chairs, and a collection of container plants make a private nook for two, complete with ocean view.*

LEFT: *Window boxes stretch along the railing of this backdoor landing, and pots cluster in corners. Plants include million bells (*Calibrachoa*), purple-leafed basil (*Ocimum basilicum*), coral bells (*Heuchera 'Santa Ana Cardinal'), and verbena.*

ABOVE: *At the height of summer, a lush green and white garden blocks a view of the busy street below and fills this balcony with serenity and scent. Plants include roses, geraniums, boxwood, and lilies.*

RIGHT: *Sometimes a railing is the star of the show. This curvaceous gem, spilling over with red geraniums and silvery licorice plant (Helichrysum petiolare), would catch eyes in any neighborhood.*

A Pint-Size Kitchen Garden

Even the tiniest balcony can produce bumper crops of vegetables, fruits, and herbs. And because many edible plants look as good as they taste, your miniplot can be as beautiful as any ornamental garden. To make the most of the small space, choose compact varieties that are well suited to your growing conditions and climate.

BEFORE

A crazy-quilt mixture of colors enlivens the formerly bland space. Careful arrangement of pots allows just enough space for a chair and tiny table, so the gardener can survey her domain from indoors or out. African daisies (Arctotis 'Safari Pink') brighten up the railing.

A console table makes a clever focal point at one end. Herbs crowd the drawers and top, while pots planted with Spanish lavender (Lavandula stoechas 'Otto Quast') afford much-needed privacy. Tomatoes, peppers, and a dwarf citrus, 'Lisbon Lemon', stand ready for picking.

BARE TO BOUNTIFUL

This tiny, bare-bones balcony reflected the plight of many apartment and condo dwellers: no privacy, no character, and no ground whatsoever. Now, though, what was nothing but an elevated concrete slab has become a lush garden brimming with fruits, vegetables, herbs, and cutting flowers. What's more, this small garden puts dinner makings only steps away from the kitchen and screens the view of, and from, neighboring units.

FACING PAGE, BOTTOM: *A small stepladder has been retrofitted with boards on the bottom treads to make room for 'Bright Lights' Swiss chard. Herbs and flowers soften the corner and blur the distinction between the balcony and the wooded landscape beyond.*

Container Winners

When growing space is limited, look for vegetables that have eye appeal as well as great flavor. Here's a small sampling.

- EGGPLANT 'Bambino' (1-inch dark purple fruit), 'Applegreen' (small, oval, light green), and 'Tango' (white, cylindrical, 7 inches long) are all good choices.

- PEPPERS Choose a novel color such as 'Purple Beauty' or 'Sweet Chocolate', or go with miniature red 'Baby Belle' or 'Jingle Bells'. On the hot side, try 'Super Cayenne' or 'Hungarian Yellow Wax Hot'.

- POTATOES All potatoes have attractive foliage, but 'All Blue' also gives you blue flowers—plus tubers that are blue inside and out, with a rich, nutlike flavor. Other winners include 'All Red' (red inside and out), 'Donna' (red skin with yellow flesh), and 'Huckleberry' (beet-colored skin with red and white marbled flesh).

- TOMATOES 'Patio' and 'Tiny Tim' are perfect for containers; 'Tumbler' is especially bred for hanging baskets.

- SWISS CHARD Plant 'Bright Lights'. Aside from delicate flavor and crunchy texture, it has bright green leaves and a mixture of stem colors: red, white, pink, yellow, and bright orange.

CHAPTER SIX

Container Plant Projects

SOME OF THE MOST EFFECTIVE PLANTINGS are the simplest— single, beautiful plants in exactly the right containers. Certainly those are the easiest design schemes to pull off successfully. But once the container-gardening bug bites, you may find the artist within clamoring for a bigger say in the goings-on. When that happens, there's only one thing to do: give in. ∾ Every artist needs inspiration, though, and that's where this chapter comes in. In these pages you'll find ideas and simple directions for container projects large and small. Follow them to a T if you like, develop variations on the themes, or merely use them as a springboard for your own improvisations. ∾ If you're just starting out in the game of artful combining, there's one thing to keep in mind. When you start with cell-pack seedlings, visualizing the end product can be difficult. So instead, go for instant lushness by using plants that are mature enough to fill out the container right from the start.

Cast-concrete boxes, custom-tinted to resemble limestone, make an elegant addition to a travertine stone patio (see page 94 for plant information).

Front and Center

Looking for a centerpiece that goes beyond cut flowers and candles? Try one of these all-but-instant projects.

SHAPING UP

This one-dimensional "topiary" heart could declare your love of gardening, or it could represent a valentine—one in a series of holiday-themed creations. To make it, first order an undivided flat of baby's tears *(Soleirolia soleirolii)* from your local nursery. Make an outline with string or set a heart-shaped stencil or cake pan on top, and then use a sharp knife to cut around the form, removing excess plants outside it as you go. Very carefully lift the heart from the flat and press it into a container filled with potting mix fortified with slow-release fertilizer. When your topiary is not performing at the dinner table, keep it in a shady spot. As the baby's tears grow beyond the outline, trim them back.

Design: Jill Slater

QUILTING CLASS

Whether on a table, wall, or bed, a patchwork quilt is a classic show-stopper. Here is one that actually grows. The only "makings" are a flat, square container 3 to 5 inches high, potting mix, and cell packs of three different low-growing ground covers. This container features *Dichondra micrantha* (upper right and lower left in the container) and Irish moss *(Sagina subulata)* for the square patches, and *Dymondia margaretae* for the center strip. Simply spread enough potting mix on the bottom of the container to ensure that the plants' crowns will be just below the top edge. Then remove the plants from their cells and press them into place inside the container.

Design: Kathleen N. Brenzel

PARTY THYME

Next time you're invited to a potluck, take along some deep-dish lemon-lime thyme. To fill a bowl that's 13 inches wide by 4½ inches deep, you'll need two 4-inch pots each of lemon and lime thyme (*Thymus × citriodorus, T. × c.* 'Lime'), and a six-pack or two of common thyme (*T. vulgaris*). Before planting, set a terra-cotta candle holder with a hurricane shade (not shown here) in the center of the bowl. Add potting mix and plants. The finishing touch is a candle with a light citrus scent.

Design: Kathleen N. Brenzel

A TABLE TO GO

When plants on the tabletop won't pack the visual punch you want, try this project. Fill an old wheelbarrow to within 3 inches of the rim with potting mix, position a few ceramic or glass tiles on the surface, and plant your choice of greenery around them. Irish moss is shown at left, but any low-growing, spreading plant would work, such as Corsican mint (*Mentha requienii*) or pennyroyal (*M. pulegium*). For after-dark interest, tuck in a few white flowers, such as the geraniums (*Pelargonium* 'Alba') shown at left; white sweet alyssum (*Lobularia maritima*) would add aromatic interest.

Design: Jill Slater

Carefree Combinations

*If you're timid about combining varied shapes, textures, and
sizes in a pot, study the groupings on these pages and note what
makes them work. Then copy the combinations if you like, or
aim for similar results with different plant material.*

1 ANNUAL MALLOW
(*Lavatera trimestris* 'Mont Blanc')

2 PURPLE SWAN RIVER DAISY
(*Brachyscome*)

3 PINK
(*Dianthus*)

4 WHITE–EDGED PURPLE PANSY
(*Viola*)

5 LICORICE PLANT
(*Helichrysum petiolare*)

THE MAGIC OF COLOR

This pot holds five different kinds of plants, yet the effect is simple
and serene. The secret is a limited color palette. Annual mallow
spreads a white cloud over a band of purple with just a tiny jolt of
hot pink. Silvery licorice plant softens the composition as it tumbles
over the edge.

Design: Teena Garay

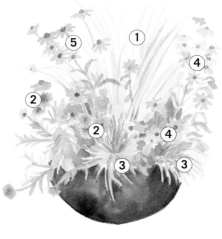

1 MEXICAN FEATHER GRASS
  (*Nassella tenuissima*)

2 BLANKET FLOWER
  (*Gaillardia × grandiflora*)

3 COMMON BLUE FESCUE
  (*Festuca glauca*)

4 GLORIOSA DAISY
  (*Rudbeckia hirta*)

5 PURPLE CONEFLOWER
  (*Echinacea purpurea*)

A NATURAL BEAUTY

When in doubt about assembling a winning combination, look to nature. Here, prairie grasses and wildflowers team up in a stone bowl 18 inches wide by 9 inches deep. Another key to the success of this composition is the bowl's dark color, which intensifies the jewel-like tones of the plants.

Design: Kathleen N. Brenzel

KEEP IT COOL

In the ground or in a pot, a green and white garden flaunts a cool sophistication. Spires of white foxglove (*Digitalis purpurea* 'Foxy') stand tall above calla lilies (*Zantedeschia rehmanii* 'Crystal Blush'), variegated English ivy *(Hedera helix),* and variegated licorice plant (*Helichrysum petiolare* 'Variegatum'). And here's proof that you can combine practicality with elegant good looks: what appears to be a stunning terra-cotta pot is actually a plastic replica, complete with "water" and "fertilizer" marks.

Design: Jill Slater

Containers Multiplied

One well-designed container combination is exactly that. Gather three or more compatible combinations together, though, and you have a garden that happens to be in containers. Here's a trio of excellent and varied examples.

1   HEN AND CHICKS
    (*Echeveria elegans*)

2   *E.* 'Morning Light'

3   *E. moranii*

4   *E.* 'Violet Queen'

5   *E. lilacina*

6   *E.* 'Colorata'

7   × *Graptoveria* 'Fred Ives'

8   STONECROP
    (*Sedum dasyphyllum*)

MADE TO ORDER

These succulents, including a half-dozen *Echeveria* species, are as well suited to their broad, shallow bowl as they are to the climate and the architecture of this southwestern patio. The massing of identical containers around a focal-point tree makes this garden a design standout.

ALL IN THE WASH

A wash of identical color unifies a trio of containers. The subdued tones of the plantings help, too. The pedestal pot holds a boxwood topiary (*Buxus microphylla japonica* 'Green Beauty') underplanted with white petunias. A clump of pink border penstemon (*Penstemon × gloxinioides* 'Apple Blossom') performs solo in the urn. Sharing honors in the rectangular planter are a pastel peony *(Paeonia)* and a pink-flowered indigo bush *(Indigofera incarnata)* underplanted with variegated English ivy *(Hedera helix)*.
Design: Jill Slater

RIGHT IN STEP

The color scheme is cool and soothing; the pots classic, clean-lined terra-cotta; and the plants old-time favorites—fuchsias and petunias—as well as bacopa *(Sutera cordata)*. The resulting container garden is the perfect complement to the time-worn stone stairs on which it sits.

93

Window Dressing

When you want to add pizzazz to a house quickly, nothing beats a window box brimming with lush plants. But that trick is not limited to windows. Window boxes work their charms just as well when they're hung on railings or lined up along the edge of a patio.

1 CARDINAL FLOWER
   (Lobelia cardinalis)

2 *Cosmos bipinnatus*

3 *Zinnia elegans* 'Envy',
   'Peter Pan Princess'

4 PETUNIA

5 SWEET POTATO VINE
   (Ipomoea batatas 'Blackie')

6 BACOPA
   (Sutera cordata)

7 SWAN RIVER DAISY
   (Brachyscome)

AN ALL-STAR CAST

Window boxes that are stars in themselves, such as these expansive cast-concrete models, call for dramatic plantings. Placed beneath room-height windows, these selections put on a colorful show all summer long in shades of rosy red, deep pink, lime green, and white.

Designs: Jill Slater (plants), Lynn Hollyn (concrete containers)

1 SAGE
(*Salvia × sylvestris*)

2 PETUNIA

3 SWAN RIVER DAISY
(*Brachyscome*)

4 GARDEN VERBENA

5 VARIEGATED LICORICE
PLANT
(*Helichrysum petiolare*
'Variegatum')

6 SPIDER PLANT
(*Chlorophytum comosum*)

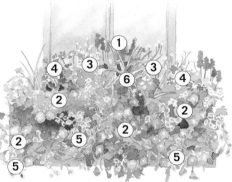

OUTSIDE THE BOX

Flowers and foliage in watery shades of gray-green, lavender-blue, purple, and white tumble from a window box—all but hiding the container in the process. The contents are simple and easy to grow.

WHAT WINDOW?

Who says window boxes are for windows only? This one, filled with a collection of pungent herbs, offers nourishment for all the senses. Shown in the photo from left to right: curry plant (*Helichrysum italicum*), sage (*Salvia officinalis*), variegated sage, and curly-leafed French parsley (*Petroselinum crispum*).

Potting Up Strawberries

No edible plants look more beautiful or grow better in containers than strawberries. Here are two ways to pot up a crop of this classic summertime treat.

STRAWBERRY JAR

Start with a pot that is at least 16 inches high (anything smaller will dry out too quickly). Choose a berry variety that performs well in your area (ask for recommendations at a good local nursery). You'll also need potting mix fortified with slow-release fertilizer, a piece of 1- to 2-inch-diameter PVC pipe to make a watering tube, and a cap to cover one end of the tube. Then follow these simple steps:

1 Cut the PVC pipe so that one end will be even with the pot's rim when it is placed vertically inside. Cap it on one end. Drill ½-inch-diameter holes about 1 inch apart along alternate sides of the pipe.

2 Partially fill the pot with soil, and insert the watering tube, capped end down, near the center. Add more potting mix, loosely filling the jar to the rim.

3 Working from the bottom up, tuck a strawberry plant into each pocket, adding soil around the roots as needed, and soaking the soil well.

4 Keep the plants in as much sun as they'll tolerate without drying out too rapidly, especially when berries are ripening. Feed once a month with a liquid organic fertilizer, and water whenever the top inch of soil feels dry—once a day in hot weather. To irrigate evenly, slip a funnel into the top of the PVC pipe and pour water into it; the holes will distribute moisture throughout the pot.

FILL SOME BASKETS

To put your crop at eye level—and beyond the reach of snails and slugs—grow your strawberries in hanging baskets. To make one like this, you'll need about 24 strawberry plants, potting mix enriched with slow-release fertilizer, a 16-inch wire basket, and a liner. You can purchase a green polyester-and-plastic version, or use either coir fiber or damp sphagnum moss.

Set 18 plants into the basket's sides, inserting them through the moss or through 3-inch slits in the liner. Add enough fertilizer-enriched potting mix to reach just below the rim and set in the remaining six plants. Follow the same care guidelines described for the strawberry pot.

Strawberries 101

There are dozens of varieties of strawberries, but they all fall into one of three types.

- June bearers form buds in the fall, then produce a single crop of fruit over a period of about six weeks beginning in late spring. In northern parts of the country, that's usually June; in warm climates, it's earlier. 'Honeoye', 'Surecrop', and 'Earliglow' are all flavorful, hardy, and resistant to the diseeases that most commonly plague strawberry plants.

- Day-neutrals bloom and bear fruit pretty much continuously from spring to fall, as long as temperatures remain between 35 and 85°F/2 and 29°C. 'Tristar' produces a cascade of fruit and foliage that make it ideal for hanging baskets. 'Tribute' offers excellent disease resistance and big crops of plump, flavorful fruit.

- Everbearers, contrary to their name, do not bear fruit all season long. Rather, they produce one crop in late spring (June in most places) and another in fall. 'Ogallala' and 'Fort Laramie' perform well anywhere, but they are especially good choices in cold or dry climates.

- Regardless of type, the best strawberries to grow are the ones that taste best to you. Sample different varieties at neighbors' homes, local farmers' markets, and pick-your-own berry farms.

Hanging Baskets

In private and public spaces alike, hanging baskets are a classic part of the summertime scene. Here are some new takes on the theme.

1 PINK POLKA-DOT PLANT
   (*Hypoestes phyllostachya*)

2 SILVER FERN
   (*Pityrogramma calomelanos*)

3 WHITE SWEET ALYSSUM
   (*Lobularia maritima*)

4 *Pilea depressa* 'Tigers Eyes'

5 AUTUMN FERN
   (*Dryopteris erythrosora*)

6 PURPLE-LEAF OXALIS

7 *Microlepia splendens*

8 DWARF CUP FLOWER
   (*Nierembergia caerulea*
   'Purple Robe')

9 PURPLE SWEET ALYSSUM
   (*Lobularia maritima*)

10 IMPATIENS, NEW GUINEA
   HYBRIDS

11 BABY'S TEARS
   (*Soleirolia soleirolii*)

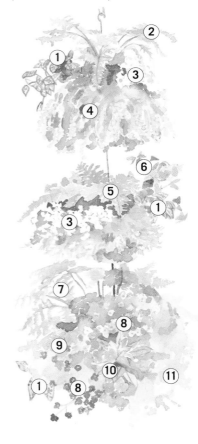

STACK 'EM UP

When planting space is at a premium—or you simply want to pack a lot of color into one small spot—try this moss-lined triple decker. You can buy ready-made triads, but if you can't find one, simply purchase small, medium, and large wire baskets. Then plant each one in the normal way (see the instructions for planting a hanging basket on page 97) and connect them with rust-proof chain.

Design: Bud Stuckey

1 COLEUS

2 FLOSS FLOWER
(*Ageratum houstonianum*)

3 AMETHYST FLOWER
(*Browallia speciosa*
'Blue Bells Improved')

4 WHITE FIBROUS BEGONIA

5 MAGENTA IMPATIENS

6 DEAD NETTLE
(*Lamium maculatum*)

7 WHITE IMPATIENS

HOLD ON

Hanging baskets don't have to dangle from above.
They look just as stunning mounted on walls or,
like this colorful number, on a lattice-trimmed pillar.
To make your own, start with a wire-mesh basket
that's flat on one side, fit it with a liner, and insert
your plants.
Design: Hilda Schwerin

A REAL COOL TRIO

This seldom-seen combo adds a cool touch to a late-
summer day—and it can sail right through the winter
in a very mild climate. The stars: white ornamental
cabbage 'Northern Lights', Scotch heather (*Calluna
vulgaris*), and variegated English ivy (*Hedera helix*).
Design: John Glover

Water Gardens

Water works magic in a garden, reflecting light, intensifying any aromas, and—even in a tiny container—relaxing both body and spirit.

A MINI LILY POND

Pink and white miniature water lilies (*Nymphaea* 'James Brydon' and *N.* 'Marliacea Albida') share this "pond" with water lettuce *(Pistia stratiotes),* variegated yellow flag iris (*Iris pseudacorus* 'Variegata'), water canna *(Canna glauca),* and soft rush *(Juncus effusus).* This garden needs full sun to perform its best; in less light, the water lily plants will still thrive, but the flowers will not open fully.

HOW SWEET IT IS

Convinced that you don't have a wet green thumb? Try this time-honored trick from Lafayette, Louisiana, where sugar mills—and sugar-kettle water gardens like this one—salted the landscape. Just fill a large glazed ceramic or metal pot with water, and then add a few pots of water plants. The ones shown here are water hyacinth *(Eichhornia crassipes),* Louisiana iris, and cast-iron plant *(Aspidistra elatior).* Set the pots on bricks or pebbles so that they rest at the proper water level (see the instructions on the facing page).
Design: Scott Daigre

MAKE YOUR OWN WATER GARDEN

To make your own water garden, all you need are a nonporous container (such as the ceramic bowl at right), clean rocks and pebbles, and naturally small plants that thrive in wet soil or an aquatic environment. Garden centers and water-garden nurseries can recommend both plants and equipment suited to your climate and your site.

Design: Jill Slater

1 Set the container in its intended site and fill the bottom with rocks.

2 Place the plants, in their pots, on the rocks. For a decorative twist, the yellow-eyed grass *(Sisyrinchium californicum)* is in its own ceramic container (see step 3 for a list of the plants in this water garden). Add or remove pebbles as needed so that the plants will stand in water of the depth they need (consult the instructions that come with the plants when you purchase them).

3 Fill the container with water almost to the rim. To prevent too-rapid evaporation, try to keep your water garden out of direct sun. This water garden features (clockwise from the top): yellow-eyed grass, *Houttuynia cordata* 'Variegata', parrot feather *(Myriophyllum aquaticum),* and water hyacinth.

CHAPTER SEVEN

Care and Maintenance

DESIGNING THE CONTAINER GARDEN of your dreams, and then shopping for exactly the right plants, pots, and accessories, can be a lot of fun. So can modestly accepting the "oohs" and "aahs" of admiring visitors. But no garden will remain praiseworthy for long without care and attention, and it's a fact of horticultural life that plants in containers need more TLC than identical versions planted in the ground. They need more feeding, watering, and pruning. They need more coddling during heat waves, cold snaps, high winds, and whatever else Mother Nature tosses our way. ⌒ *That's the bad news. The good news is that the burgeoning interest in container gardening has led to a multitude of products that make potted-plant tending easier than ever before. That includes everything from dwarf trees that are bred to thrive in close confines to slow-release fertilizers that feed your plants on demand to watering systems that deliver exactly the right amount of water, whether you're around or not.*

High-quality tools can make container-gardening chores easier and faster.

Watering

Watering is the single most important job in caring for your container garden. Because plants in containers have a limited amount of soil from which to draw moisture, they dry out much faster than their in-ground counterparts.

WHEN TO WATER

How do you know when your plants need moisture? This easy trick works in most cases: poke your finger into the top inch of soil; if it feels dry, the plant needs watering. But that's not a universal guideline. Some plants need soil that stays evenly moist, while others fare better in drier conditions. Ask about the needs of specific plants at the nursery where you purchase them, or consult a gardening book.

Plant preferences aside, there are a few general rules. For instance, lightweight potting mixes dry out faster than heavier ones. Plants in hanging baskets dry out faster than potted versions on the ground. Porous containers lose moisture more quickly than nonporous ones, and small pots, regardless of material, require more frequent watering than large ones.

Weather plays a part, too. Plants nearly always need extra watering in hot, dry, or windy conditions. In very hot weather, you may need to water two or three times a day.

HOW TO WATER

When you water, fully saturate the soil; don't just moisten the top few inches. You've done the job right when water runs freely from the drainage hole. When watering a container without a drain, add water equal to about one-quarter the volume of soil.

When a saucer under a container is full, empty it right away if you can. If that's not possible, at least drain it within 24 hours; water that's allowed to stand much longer will keep the soil soggy. (Use a bulb-type baster to remove water from saucers under big containers.)

BELOW: *Watering plants with an old-fashioned can is a relaxing pastime with a practical advantage: when you look at each plant close-up every day, you can spot small problems before they become big ones.*

LEFT: *A watering wand on the end of a hose lets you reach hanging baskets easily.* RIGHT: *Submersing pots in a tub of water for a 30-minute soak can be a lifesaver in hot weather.*

Drainage Solutions

Getting water into and out of a container to ensure well-drained soil is always a concern. Below are two easy fixes.

WHEN WATER DOESN'T DRAIN ... chances are the drainage hole is blocked. Turn the pot on its side (or as far over as you can get it) and push a pointed stick or large nail into the opening to clear the blockage in the hole.

WHEN WATER DRAINS TOO FAST ... the potting mix has probably dried out so much that it has shrunk away from the container walls. If the pot is small enough, submerge it in a tub of water for about half an hour. Otherwise, set a hose on the soil surface near the base of the plant and adjust the flow to a trickle. Let the water run until the soil in the container is fully saturated.

WAYS AND MEANS

There are numerous ways to deliver needed moisture to your plants. The best method for you depends on the size and location of your container garden and on your own routine. No matter what watering equipment you choose, always apply the water in a gentle stream, drip, or spray; a strong flow can displace soil and damage plant roots.

WATERING CAN Watering each pot as needed may be your choice if you have a small garden or if you simply enjoy puttering. If so, use a can that has a "rose"—a sprinkler head that fits onto the spout.

GARDEN HOSE Attach a flow head that will deliver a gentle trickle to the soil surface or, bet-ter yet, use a watering wand with a rose like the ones made for watering cans. One caution: water from a hose that's been baking in the sun can be hot enough to damage plants; before watering, let the hose run until the water is fairly cool.

SUBMERSION For hanging baskets and small pots, watering by submersion is a real time-saver. A good soak in the morning can keep soil moist all day or revive plants when their potting soil has become dangerously dry. Simply lower the pot into a tub of water (covering the pot rim but not the plant itself) and keep it there for about half an hour. A periodic dunk is also good for terra-cotta pots, which tend to dry out even in mild weather.

SELF-WATERING POTS

Catalogs and garden centers sell containers with built-in reservoirs that deliver consistent moisture to the soil. You still need to fill the reservoir, of course, but depending on the weather and the size of the container, you can go for many weeks between refills. If you don't care for the look of plastic, you can put these pots inside other, more elegant containers, as long as you leave room to reach the holes to fill them.

DRIP IRRIGATION

A drip system delivers water to individual containers through a network of thin tubes and emitters. You customize the layout according to your needs, and the water goes directly into each plant's root zone with little moisture loss to evaporation or runoff, and no harmful fluctuations in soil moisture. A simple automated system can make watering effortless, reduce your water bill, and help your plants grow lush and full.

INSTALLING A BASIC DRIP SYSTEM

If you already have an automatic watering system for your lawn, it's usually a simple matter to add another valve for your container system. Failing that, you need only connect the system to an existing hose bibb, using a Y attachment so that you can still connect a standard garden hose. You can add an automatic timer or operate the system manually. If you choose the former approach, look for a controller that lets you run the system several times a day; that's a big plus in hot, dry, or windy weather.

The main line. Use either ⅜- or ½-inch-diameter black polyethylene tubing to take water from the valve to your container garden, and conceal it any way you can. Don't take it too far, though, or you'll risk uneven water distribution. A ⅜-inch line should extend less than 100 feet; a ½-inch line can safely go to just under 200 feet.

Into the pots. Run ¼-inch vinyl minitubing from the main line into each container. For containers that you seldom move, you can run the tubing up through the drainage hole; otherwise, take it up the side and over the lip. For hanging baskets, run the microtubing up the wall or a post and across to the basket's hanger wire. To prevent backflow on hanging baskets, put an atmospheric breaker on the line 6 inches above the highest emitter, or simply keep all emitters 2 inches away from the foliage or soil.

Running the system. You'll need to experiment to find the optimum running time for your garden. Start by turning it on for 5 minutes, and then check the results. A container is properly watered when the soil is wet and some water is coming from the drainage holes. If water streams out, it means you've run the system too long. If no water emerges and the soil is not thoroughly wet, you need to let the water flow longer or replace your emitters with larger ones.

This hanging-basket emitter is actually a 2- to 4-gallon-per-hour mister that sprays both soil and foliage. Bonsai wire holds the tubing in place and keeps the mister head aimed in the right direction.

A basic drip system consists of a backflow prevention device—in this case, an automatic antisiphon valve (A)— a filter (B), a pressure regulator (C), and a compression fitting (D). The automatic controller (E) operates the system, and a T fitting above the shutoff valve (F) accommodates a hose bibb.

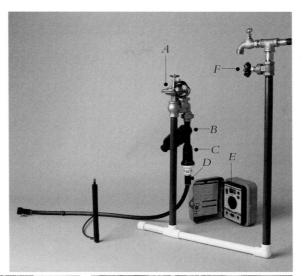

A pot up to 10 inches wide needs only a single emitter. Here, an elbow fitting takes the tubing over the pot edge at a 90-degree angle; a U stake holds tubing and emitter in place.

Two emitters will suffice for pots that measure 10 to 15 inches across. Above, a notched stake holds the tubing in place, and the emitters are attached to a T fitting.

Large pots can be handled in a couple of ways. Here, tubing with factory-installed emitters encircles a plant. U stakes hold the emitter line in place.

Another good option for big pots is a multi-outlet emitter, sometimes called a "bubbler." The head can be adjusted to change the spray.

Save That Water!

Whether water is in short supply where you live or you simply want to spend less time watering, you can take some simple steps to reduce your plants' thirst:

- Mulch the soil surface with pebbles, bark, or compost.
- Put one container inside of another; fill the space between with damp peat moss or coir fiber, and cover the whole surface with small pebbles.
- Group pots closely together so that they shelter and provide shade for one another.
- In a hot climate or when a heat wave strikes, provide a source of shade during the hottest part of the day.
- Use the largest possible containers that are appropriate for your plants; the more soil a pot contains, the more slowly it will dry out.
- Select unthirsty plants. In particular, look for plants that are native to dry climates.
- When you plant or replant, use soil polymers in your potting mix. They hold on to both water and dissolved nutrients, keeping them readily available to plant roots. You can buy commercial potting mixes with gel already added or mix it in yourself. (If you mix it, use the manufacturer's recommended proportions; see page 13 for more information.)

Feeding

Plants in the ground can send their roots deep into the soil in search of nutrients. But potted plants depend on you to supply nourishment. If you're a novice gardener, that chore can seem daunting when you first glimpse a garden center's bewildering array of fertilizers. Fortunately, keeping your plants well fed is much simpler than it may appear.

TYPES OF FERTILIZER

Fertilizers come in two basic types: inorganic/chemical and organic/natural. Both types are available in all-purpose plant foods as well as specialty formulas for plants such as roses, citrus trees, and acid-loving shrubs.

INORGANIC/CHEMICAL FERTILIZERS

These fertilizers are made from synthetic substances that contain highly concentrated amounts of specific nutrients—primarily nitrogen, phosphorus, and potassium. When you apply an inorganic fertilizer, you see almost instant results because the nutrients are immediately available to your plants. This quick fix is perfect for times when you want to make a big impact in a hurry, such as for temporary displays of flowering annuals, or for giving perennials a fast start.

ORGANIC/NATURAL FERTILIZERS

These fertilizers don't feed your plants directly. Rather, they add essential nutrients, major and minor, to the soil, where they become available to the plants' roots. Organic fertilizers are made from the remains or by-products of living or once-living

organisms. Manure, fish emulsion, bonemeal, and kelp meal are all examples of organic fertilizers that can be used alone or in various combinations.

In addition to providing essential nutrients, organic fertilizers improve the structure of the soil, thereby allowing water and oxygen to move freely.

Organic fertilizers tend to work more slowly than inorganics, but they're longer lasting. This soil-building staying power makes them ideal for use with trees, shrubs, and long-lived perennials—or for large planters in which you keep the same soil from year to year.

Edible plants, too, benefit from organic fertilizers. Many gardeners swear that vegetables grown with organic fertilizers taste better than their chemically grown counterparts. And university studies have shown that the organically grown versions do contain more nutrients.

DIETARY TROUBLESHOOTING

Often, the first signs of a nutrient deficiency—major or minor—appear in a plant's leaves. Here are some symptoms to watch for. In each case, your local nursery can recommend a foliar spray (see "Liquid Fertilizers" on page 109) to solve the immediate problem and a fertilizer supplement for long-term care.

LEAF SYMPTOMS	DEFICIENCY
Yellow and smaller than normal; on some plants they may turn red or purple. Overall growth is stunted or dwarfed.	Nitrogen
Small, with edges scorched, purplish, or blue-green in color. May fall early. Overall growth is reduced and weakened; flower and fruit production diminished.	Phosphorus
Tips and edges are yellow and scorched-looking, with brownish-purple spotting underneath.	Potassium
Turn dark from the base outward and die.	Calcium
Yellow between the veins; veins remain green or slightly yellow.	Iron
Leaf centers are reddish or yellow; dead spots appear between the veins.	Magnesium
Upper leaves are yellow in the center, between the veins, with no sign of red.	Manganese
Veins are lighter in color than the tissue in between.	Sulfur

Both chemical and organic fertilizers come in liquid and dry forms to meet a variety of plants' nutritional needs.

FORMS OF FERTILIZER

You'll find both organic and inorganic fertilizers in two basic forms: dry and liquid. Whichever kind you choose, follow the package directions and don't be tempted to toss in a little extra "for good measure." Too much fertilizer all at once—especially the potent chemical kinds—can do harm to your plants.

DRY FERTILIZERS Dry varieties come in both traditional powders and granules and the newer timed/controlled-release capsules. The latter are a real boon to container gardeners. You mix the fertilizer into the potting mix at planting time, and a small amount of nutrients diffuses into the soil with each watering. When necessary throughout the growing season, you can scratch more capsules into the surface. They remain active for varying lengths of time, usually from about 3 to 8 months.

LIQUID FERTILIZERS Choose from crystals, granules, or liquid concentrates that you mix with water, and apply with a hose, watering can, or spray bottle.

The spray types, known as "foliar feeds," are generally used to deliver instant supplies of specific nutrients, either on a routine basis or to correct deficiencies.

PLANT NUTRITION

All plants require the same basic "big three" nutrients—nitrogen, phosphorous, and potassium—as well as various secondary minerals and trace elements. But how often they need them, and in what proportions, can vary. Most plants need regular feedings from spring through summer or early autumn, when they're actively growing, and none from mid- to late autumn through winter, when they are dormant. Containers filled with multiple plants may need extra fertilizer.

DOING THE NUMBERS The three-number formulas on fertilizer labels represent the percentage by weight of nitrogen (N), phosphorus (P), and potassium (K). For instance, 5–10–5 fertilizer contains 5 percent nitrogen, 10 percent phosphorous, and 5 percent potassium. Each element is essential for a different aspect of growth. Nitrogen supplies the power for leaf and stem growth. That's why too much of it can make plants overly lush and leafy. Phosphorus promotes strong, vigorous roots and the formation of flowers, fruits, and seeds. Potassium supports all phases of growth and helps plants control aphids.

Tea Time

One of the best liquid fertilizers is a simple brew that you can easily make yourself: compost tea. Not only does it provide balanced nutrition, but evidence indicates that it can also help prevent plant diseases. All you need are a bucket and some compost. If you don't have access to a fresh supply, a high-quality commercial version will work fine. To make the tea:

- Fill a bucket about one-third of the way with compost.
- Add water to fill the bucket, and let it steep for 3 to 4 days.
- Strain the mixture through cheesecloth. (Return the solids to your compost bin or add them to the soil in one of your containers.)
- Before using the brew, dilute it to the color of weak tea. Apply as you would any liquid fertilizer.
- To use compost tea as a foliar feed, add $1/8$ teaspoon of vegetable oil or mild dishwashing liquid to each gallon of tea. This will help the solution adhere to plants' foliage. One caution: strong sunlight can damage the wet leaves, so do your spraying in the morning or on an overcast day.

Trees, Shrubs, and Perennials

Annuals are quick-change artists, allowing you to play with color, form, and texture as your mood decrees (as you have seen in earlier chapters). But for structure and a sense of permanence in a garden—even one with all its roots in containers—look to trees, shrubs, and hardy perennials. With proper care these long-lived plants can thrive in pots for years.

TREES

The best trees for containers are small, slow-growing, and tidy in habit, with compact root systems. Steer clear of varieties that drop large quantities of leaves, seed heads, or messy fruits throughout the growing season. On the other hand, do look for trees with year-round charms such as fragrant spring blooms, colorful autumn foliage, bird-enticing berries, and distinctive branching patterns that hold their appeal even after leaves have dropped. And, of course, choose a variety that's suited to your climate and the growing conditions in your garden.

Like any other plants, trees vary in their shade tolerance and their ability to withstand such common hazards as high winds, air pollution, and salt spray. Some of the best candidates are too tender to remain outdoors year-round except in mild climates. And if you live where winters get very cold, you will have to move any contained tree to protected territory (see page 124).

Use a container with plenty of room for root growth and for staking a young tree, if that's a temporary necessity. In general, 18 to 20 inches across and 16 to 24 inches deep is the minimum size you'll need to start. (Keep in mind that you always want to have about 1 to 2 inches of open soil on all sides of the root ball.) As the tree grows, you can either trim its roots and refresh the soil, or move up to a larger pot.

In most parts of the country, spring is the best time for tree planting (in containers or otherwise). Where winters are mild, you can do the job any time from early autumn to midwinter.

Apply a balanced fertilizer once in spring and again in summer. Withhold fertilizer as autumn approaches; it will spur tender new growth that is vulnerable to killing frosts.

A trio of dwarf Alberta spruce trees coexists happily in a planter with English ivy (Hedera helix).

Good Container Trees

CONIFERS
Dwarf Alberta spruce (*Picea glauca albertiana* 'Conica')
Japanese red pine (*Pinus densiflora* 'Umbraculifera')
Nordmann fir (*Abies nordmanniana*)
Norfolk Island pine (*Araucaria heterophylla*)
Scotch pine (*Pinus sylvestris* 'French Blue')
Weeping Atlantic cedar (*Cedrus atlantica* 'Glauca Pendula')

BROAD-LEAFED EVERGREENS
American holly (*Ilex opaca*)
English holly (*Ilex aquifolium*)
Evergreen pear (*Pyrus kawakamii*)
Strawberry tree (*Arbutus unedo*)
Sweet bay (*Laurus nobilis*)
Sweet olive (*Osmanthus fragrans*)

DECIDUOUS TREES
Eastern redbud (*Cercis canadensis*)
Flowering cherry, flowering plum (*Prunus*)
Japanese maple (*Acer palmatum*)
Japanese snowdrop tree (*Styrax japonicus*)
Star magnolia (*Magnolia stellata*)
Vine maple (*Acer circinatum*)

CLOCKWISE FROM TOP LEFT: *Japanese maple, strawberry tree, star magnolia, vine maple, English holly*

POTTED FRUIT TREES

Many fruit trees, as well as fruit-bearing shrubs and vines, can prosper in containers. For the most part, these plants require the same basic care as their strictly ornamental counterparts. As always, though, learn as much as you can about the specific needs of your choices before you offer them a home in a pot.

Nearly all standard fruit trees come in dwarf forms that produce full-size crops, including apple, apricot, cherry, nectarine, peach, pear, and plum. Bear in mind, though, that in many cases you will need two different varieties to ensure pollination. The nursery staff or catalog can advise you on which varieties make the best combinations.

Dwarf citrus trees, including orange, lemon, lime, kumquat, and calamondin (a kumquat–mandarin orange hybrid), are excellent candidates for container growing. In northern gardens they thrive outdoors all summer and then sail right through the winter in a sunny window.

Trees are not your only fruit options, though. If you choose your varieties carefully, you can grow blueberries, raspberries, guavas, and even grapes in pots. And potted kiwi vines—both tender (*Actinidia deliciosa*) and hardy (*A. kolomikta* and *A. arguta*)—actually bloom and bear fruit faster than most of their in-ground counterparts.

SHRUBS

As with trees, the best shrubs for containers are compact, slow-growing varieties. Many popular shrubs come in dwarf versions, which often have the word "nana" in their botanical names. Plant in spring in cold-weather regions, early autumn to midwinter in warmer climates. Some shrubs need a lightweight potting mix; others perform better in heavier soil. And acid lovers, such as camellias and rhododendrons, need a special potting mix.

In general, potted shrubs perform best with a monthly application of balanced fertilizer from spring through summer. If you plant in spring or summer, wait 2 weeks before the first feeding, and don't fertilize autumn- or winter-planted shrubs until spring.

When your shrubs outgrow their pots, you have the same choices you have with trees: either move them to bigger containers or trim the roots (see page 119 for root-pruning pointers).

Favorite Container Shrubs

CONIFERS
English yew *(Taxus baccata)*
Juniperus **(Especially good choices include**
    J. conferta **'Emerald Sea',** *J. horizontalis*
    'Bar Harbor', and *J. procumbens* **'Nana')**
Mugho pine *(Pinus mugo mugo)*
Umbrella pine *(Sciadopitys verticillata)*
Weeping Norway spruce *(Picea abies*
    'Pendula')

BROAD-LEAFED EVERGREENS
Angel's trumpet *(Brugmansia)*
Boxwood *(Buxus)*
Camellia
Flowering maple *(Abutilon* **hybrids)**
Japanese aucuba *(Aucuba japonica)*
Oleander *(Nerium oleander)*
Oregon grape *(Mahonia aquifolium)*
Rhododendron

DECIDUOUS SHRUBS
Bigleaf hydrangea *(Hydrangea macrophylla)*
Butterfly bush, summer lilac *(Buddleja*
    davidii)
Daphne
Fuchsia
Japanese barberry *(Berberis thunbergii)*
Rose *(Rosa)*
Slender deutzia *(Deutzia gracilis)*
Tree peony *(Paeonia)*

CLOCKWISE FROM TOP LEFT: *Angel's trumpet, rhododendron, English yew, Japanese barberry, fuchsia, bigleaf hydrangea, Oregon grape, tree peony*

STANDARD TIME

If you want the look of a tree without the size, opt for a "standard"—a shrub or vine trained to grow on a single, upright trunk. You can buy pretrained standards or grow your own.

STAKING Choose a plant with a strong, straight main stem. Set it in a pot, along with a stake that's almost as high as the plant. Tie the stem to the stake in several places, using soft fabric strips. (No wire!)

TRIMMING Remove all side shoots up to the point where you want the foliage to start, about 3 feet above the base for most shrubs and vines. Turn the plant regularly to keep it from growing toward the sun.

PINCHING When the plant reaches the desired height, pinch off the growing tip to stop upward growth and encourage side branching. You may want to trim the crown into a rounded ball, the style that gives standards

the nickname "lollipop trees." If your standard is a vine or a climbing rose, let its stems cascade down naturally. To keep the plant from reverting to its shrubby form, remove any suckers that emerge along the trunk.

TRAINING A STANDARD

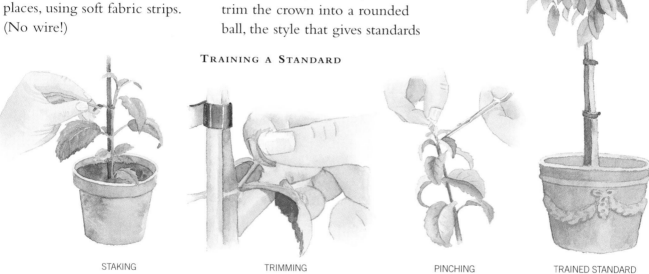

| STAKING | TRIMMING | PINCHING | TRAINED STANDARD |

Some Favorite Standards

Bottlebrush (Callistemon)
Bougainvillea
Camellia
Common heliotrope (Heliotropium arborescens)
Flowering maple (Abutilon hybrids)
Fuchsia
Hibiscus
Holly (Ilex)
Lantana
Rose (Rosa)
Rosemary (Rosmarinus officinalis)
Wisteria

CLOCKWISE FROM TOP LEFT: *Rosemary, hibiscus, camellia*

SPRING TUNE-UP

In the spring, perennials that are less than two years old, or that have been divided the previous year, benefit from a light perk-me-up. Using a screwdriver or dibble, poke three 1-inch holes about 6 to 8 inches deep in the soil (keep holes about 2 inches from the plant crowns to avoid damaging roots). Drop about a teaspoon of slow-release fertilizer into each hole and cover with soil. Then lightly scratch the soil surface (an ordinary table fork works well for this procedure) and add about 1 inch of compost.

PERENNIALS

Perennials can be stunning as the basis of a more or less permanent container garden, but unless you have the space to conceal "off-duty" plants, choose your stock carefully. Unlike annuals, which generally put out nonstop color from spring to fall, most perennials bloom in a single flush, with perhaps a second, smaller wave later on. For the biggest impact, look for varieties that have a longer-than-normal blooming period or foliage that's eye-catching even without flowers attached.

Don't cramp your perennials; most will quickly outgrow a small container long before the end of the season. If one or two newly planted specimens look lonely in a pot, surround them with lower-growing annuals to add some temporary color. Generally, an 18-inch-wide container will hold two 1-gallon plants, and a 20- to 24-inch container will hold four to five 1-gallon plants.

Perennials differ in their moisture requirements, but most need regular watering during spring and summer growth periods, and less frequent applications during the fall and the winter dormant season. Food needs, too, can vary, but as a general rule, apply a balanced fertilizer monthly during the growing season.

Unlike most perennials, herbaceous peonies, such as 'Mrs. Franklin D. Roosevelt', should not be divided. When a plant outgrows its pot, ease it out gently and move it to bigger quarters.

Perennial Pleasers

Astilbe *(Astilbe × arendsii)*
Basket-of-gold *(Aurinia saxatilis)*
Bellflower *(Campanula)*
Carnation *(Dianthus caryophyllus)*
Daylily *(Hemerocallis)*

Dead nettle, spotted nettle *(Lamium maculatum)*
Evergreen candytuft *(Iberis sempervirens)*
Fringed bleeding heart *(Dicentra eximia)*
Hosta
Pink *(Dianthus 'Allwoodii')*
Yarrow *(Achillea)*

CLOCKWISE FROM TOP LEFT: *Evergreen candytuft, daylily, yarrow, hosta, carnation*

Pruning

The reasons for pruning container plants are the same as for pruning those in the ground: to maintain the health of the plants, to increase the production of flowers or fruit, to direct growth where you want it to go, or simply to keep growth within the desired bounds.

PRUNING FOR HEALTH

The golden rule of garden health is to remove diseased, damaged, or odd-looking growth the minute you spot it, regardless of the time of year. That applies to all plants, from venerable trees to new seedlings, in the ground or in containers. Cut all the way back into healthy tissue, and unless you know the plant part is healthy (for instance, if you're pruning off a storm-damaged branch), destroy it or send it off with the trash; don't put it in the compost bin. In the case of shrubs and trees, prune out crossing or crowded branches to provide good air circulation as well as pleasing form.

PRUNING FOR PRODUCTION

A few simple procedures will ensure that your container garden puts on the longest, most prolific show possible.

ANNUALS There's a one-word secret to making annuals put on a spectacular show all summer long: deadhead. Pluck or clip off all flowers as soon as they've passed their peak—and definitely before seed heads appear. The more you pluck, the more blooms the plant will produce. The reason is simple. In biological terms, the purpose of any organism is to reproduce itself. In the case of an annual, that means when its flowers have set seed for the next generation, the plant's work is finished.

PERENNIALS Some plants produce a primary show of flowers, followed by a second, less profuse display later on. For these, cut or shear back the plants by one-half or more after the initial bloom period to encourage the best "second wave." For perennials that bloom only once, clip off spent flowers as they appear, and then at the end of the growing season cut the plant back. This will encourage compact growth and abundant bloom the following year.

To keep annuals like these petunias blooming abundantly all summer long, clip or pinch off all flowers before they set seed.

FRUIT Trees, shrubs, and vines that produce fruit vary greatly in their pruning requirements. Ask for specific guidelines at the nursery where you purchase your plants, or consult a pruning manual or fruit-growing book.

PRUNING FOR SHAPE AND SIZE

Clipping early and often encourages plants to grow in the desired direction, stay small enough to thrive in a pot, and continue to look their best year after year.

INITIAL PRUNING After planting, prune young shrubs and perennial vines to a few strong shoots, leaving two or three buds on each one. This will increase fullness and strength, and encourage the plant to grow in the desired direction. As stems get long enough, which may not be until the following season, you can tie them to their supports and begin any formal shaping (see guidelines for creating an espalier on page 67).

CONTAINMENT PRUNING Tree growth is best controlled by root pruning (see "Major Tune-Up" on page 119), but you can easily clip shrubs to keep them to a manageable size (provided you've chosen wisely to begin with). Because shrubs tend to grow vertically, with most growth occurring close to the stem tip, all you need to do is cut the

The Right Cut

Whether you're clipping spent blooms from annuals or pruning a tree limb, you always want a clean, precise cut. A ragged cut or torn stem provides easy entry for diseases and insect pests. Use sharp, good-quality pruning shears (or scissors for flower stems and thin shoots). When you're working with diseased plants, dip your shears in a 10 percent bleach and water solution after each cut to avoid spreading the problem to healthy tissue.

The angle of your cut is determined by the bud pattern of the plant.

When a plant's buds occur alternately along the shoot, cut on the diagonal just above an outward-facing bud.

For a plant with buds opposite each other, make a straight cut directly above both buds.

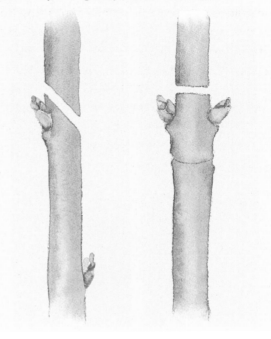

growing tips back to the appropriate length. Just be sure to leave a couple of pairs of buds on each shoot, and make your cut just above an outward-facing bud (see "The Right Cut" above).

REMEDIAL PRUNING In addition to cutting out diseased, damaged, or dead wood, it's important to remove crossing, crowded, or misshapen shoots from shrubs and trees both. Not only does this process improve your plants' appearance, but it also opens up the branch structure to permit

good air circulation—and that's essential for good health.

From time to time you may notice shoots with leaves that look different in color or shape from those on the rest of the plant. For instance, the new leaves may be solid green, when the others are variegated. Clip them off immediately. It may be that your cultivar is reverting to the color of the species it was bred from. Or perhaps the plant's stem has been grafted to the roots of an entirely different plant (normal practice with roses and fruit trees in particular).

The Show Must Go On

In a container garden, especially a small one, you want your plants to look their best throughout the growing season. Many perennials perform that task naturally; all you need to do is keep them fed and watered, and spent blooms clipped, just as you would with annuals (see "Pruning for Production" on page 116). Daylilies *(Hemerocallis)*, yarrow *(Achillea)*, false sunflowers *(Heliopsis)*, balloon flower *(Platycodon)*, hostas, and astilbes (along with numerous others) fall into this category. Some perennials, though, require a little more help to keep their youthful good looks. For these perennials, two simple techniques—shaping and shearing—can work wonders.

Perennials that bloom in a single flush, such as blue false indigo *(Baptisia australis)*, *Euphorbia polychroma*, and catmint *(Nepeta × faassenii)*, benefit from shaping. After the flowers fade, cut the foliage back by about a third to form a pleasing shape that blends well with other plants in your garden. Hedge clippers work best for this job.

Some perennials, including cranesbill *(Geranium)*, lungwort *(Pulmonaria)*, and lady's-mantle *(Alchemilla)*, can get lanky and leggy as the summer progresses. When this happens, shear the plants all the way back to the ground. Scratch a little fertilizer into the potting soil, mulch with compost, and keep the plants well watered. Within a couple of weeks, you'll have an attractive mound of new, compact foliage. And sometimes you'll be rewarded with a second flush of blossoms.

Shaping

Shearing

MOVING ON UP

If a container plant looks crowded even after being trimmed, or if a plant simply looks too big for its container, move it to a larger pot. A plant that just seems to be growing poorly, with no signs of pests or disease, is also a candidate for larger quarters (most likely it's become pot-bound). In most cases, one pot size larger is best, but fast-growing plants can go up two sizes. If the container you choose has been used before, scrub it according to the instructions on page 119 before moving in the new plant.

MAJOR TUNE-UP

After a plant has been in a container for about three years, or starts to look less than stellar, it's time to refresh it by trimming or (in the case of perennials only!) dividing the roots.

EXAMINE THE ROOT BALL If the roots of a tree or shrub are twisted and wound around the soil clump, they need to be trimmed. First, pull out and untangle large roots (soil will fall away from the root ball as you do this), then use shears or a pruning saw to cut the big roots back by a third to a half. Divide crowded perennials by slicing through the crown or, in the case of tuberous-rooted plants like daylilies or irises, through the fleshy roots.

REPOT First, clean the pot using a stiff brush and a solution of 4 parts water to 1 part household bleach; rinse the pot with clear water, and replace the drainage-hole cover with a fresh one. If you found any sign of disease or pest damage on the roots, add all-new soil. Otherwise, it's fine to combine part of the old soil with fresh mix and a healthy helping of compost. Set the plant back in the pot. Add soil to cover the roots, scratch in some slow-release fertilizer, and you should be in good shape for another three years.

BIG-TIME ROOT PRUNING

If you're faced with a tree that's too large to wrestle out of its pot, try this method in early spring. Using a narrow, very sharp shovel or spade, dig as far as you can reach into the pot along one side. Cut off clumps of old roots and remove each section from the pot. Continue until you've pruned off at least half a dozen good-size root sections from mature or pot-bound trees. Take fewer from less crowded or immature plants.

Fill the empty spaces with fresh potting mix and compost. Repeat the procedure on the opposite side of the container; leave the other two sides intact until the following spring.

Perennials need to be divided about every three years, or when they start thinning in the center or looking crowded in their pots. The procedure is simple (if somewhat messy): Start by easing the plant out of its container (1). Using a knife or sharp spade, slice through the crown (2). Pull the sections apart, keeping vigorous outer growth and discarding portions that are weak, woody, shriveled, or diseased (3). Rub some old soil off the root ball to make room for fresh potting mix, and replant the divisions in fresh containers (4).

Pests and Diseases

Diseases and pests can pay visits to any garden, even one with all its roots in containers. Fortunately, though, there is much you can do to protect your plants—without launching a spraying campaign, which would be likely to cause more harm than any pest or disease ever could.

PREVENTION

As with most problems in life, garden pests and diseases are far easier to avoid than to deal with after they've struck. Nothing can guarantee a trouble-free garden, but these tactics go a long way toward safeguarding your plants.

KEEP IT CLEAN Always use clean containers and sterile potting mix. Pull weeds, and pick up fallen fruit and dead flowers and leaves as soon as you spot them. Disease organisms and many insect pests breed or overwinter in weeds and plant litter.

KNOW YOUR PLANTS Learn what each plant needs in the way of food, water, light, winter protection, and other environmental factors. By providing optimum growing conditions, you'll keep plants healthy and better able to fend off pests and diseases.

KNOW WHEN TO SAY NO You may fall in love with a plant that would require extra care to thrive in your locale. Unless you're sure you can—and will—provide the conditions it needs, leave it at the nursery. At best, it will suffer undue stress, and stressed plants (like stressed people) tend to attract more than their share of physical problems.

PROVIDE HEALTHY SURROUNDINGS Raise your containers off the ground to provide good drainage and make them less attractive to crawling pests. Maintain enough distance between plants to allow good air circulation and adequate light. Erect or plant barriers to protect plants from harsh, drying winds. Provide adequate shelter from cold winter weather (see page 124).

KNOW YOUR ENEMY Learn how to recognize both disease symptoms and "bad bugs"; don't panic when you see either one. Many diseases are easy to remedy if caught in the early stages, and most pests cause little harm in small numbers.

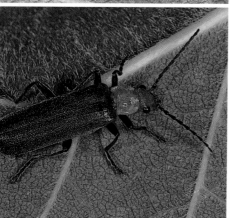

In a garden that's free of pesticides, beneficial insects and other predators can usually keep bad bug populations well under control. Shown here, clockwise from top left, are four of the hardest-charging good guys: lacewing, ladybug, tachinid fly, soldier beetle.

ENCOURAGE ALLIES Beneficial insects and other garden residents, such as birds, toads, bats, and lizards, consume many times their weight in destructive, disease-carrying pests. The most effective way to draw helpful predators to your garden is simply to not use pesticides, which kill the "good guys" along with the bad ones.

CONTROL

Usually, the most effective way to deal with larger insect pests, such as slugs, snails, caterpillars, beetles, and weevils, is to hand-pick them and drown them in a bucket of water laced with soap or alcohol. If you find that chore less than appealing, put a price on the pests' heads and hire a "posse" of young bounty hunters; most children love nothing better than insect search-and-destroy missions. To get rid of aphids, thrips, white-flies, and other small insects, simply blast them from your plants with a strong spray from a garden hose.

In the event of severe infestations, homemade sprays generally provide all the fire power you need. For instance, a spray made by mixing 2 tablespoons of dishwashing liquid in 1 gallon of warm water will kill soft-bodied insects on contact. To penetrate the hard, waxy shells of beetles and weevils, add 2 teaspoons of citrus oil or peppermint extract to the mix. Add a tablespoon or

Three for the Road

Plant diseases are caused by three types of organisms: fungi, bacteria, and viruses. Unfortunately, if the disease has progressed very far, your only option may be to destroy the plant and replace it with a new one. In the early stages, though, there is often hope. (See page 122 for some options, and for more detail on diseases and treatments, consult your Cooperative Extension Office.)

FUNGAL DISEASES are the most common by far and usually take the form of molds and mildews. Any part of a plant may be affected, and common symptoms include wilt, rot, and leaf spots. Fungal spores multiply rampantly on warm, wet leaves or stems. They overwinter in soil or in plant debris and come to life when spring rains begin. The one good thing about fungi is that they tend to spread slowly, so if you respond quickly, you stand a very good chance of saving your plants.

BACTERIA are nearly all harmless, and many are beneficial—even necessary to life. But the few disease-causing types move fast and cause serious problems, usually in the form of wilt or rot. Because most of the bacteria that attack plants can't survive in frozen soil, they cause the most damage in mild-winter climates. Unfortunately, a few destructive bacteria overwinter in the bodies of insects, which transmit the diseases to plants the following spring.

VIRUSES seldom cause serious damage, but the few real killers cause plants to suddenly wilt and die. If your plants' leaves become twisted, crinkled, or mottled, the likely cause is a virus. The tiny organisms overwinter in wild plants, and they're transmitted by insects such as aphids, whiteflies, thrips, and leafhoppers.

two of baking soda to the soap solution, and the spray will kill fungi as well as insects. Sprays made from garlic, hot pepper, and coffee are also potent pest killers. If homemade remedies are not your style, you can buy similar products at most nurseries and through many catalogs.

Two warnings, though: First, these sprays will kill beneficial insects along with the "bad" ones, so when you use them, make sure you've got the right target, and aim carefully. Second, even though a pesticide may be lethal only to insects, ingesting it could harm humans or other animals. Make sure you keep all pest-control products away from children and pets—preferably under lock and key.

MINIMIZING PESTS AND DISEASES

Even with the best preventive maintenance, pests and diseases can strike your garden. The key to minimizing damage: identify the cause and act fast. But don't overreact—you could cause more problems than you had to begin with. These pages illustrate the problems that most often plague container plants, along with your best coping mechanisms.

DOWNY MILDEW

Downy mildew rarely kills, but it can turn plants unsightly, stunted, and unproductive. Symptoms vary but often include a powdery whitish, gray, or light brown mold on the undersides of leaves. Remove and destroy infected plant parts, or entire plants if the condition has progressed far. Prevent future outbreaks by practicing good garden hygiene: clean up debris, provide good air circulation for plants, and water early in the day so that foliage dries before nightfall.

SPIDER MITES

These tiny spider relatives suck juices from leaves, stems, and flower buds. Early symptoms include stippled, spotted, bleached, or deformed tissue. One sure clue that mites are present: soft, white webbing on buds or between stems and leaf petioles. A good hosing down usually gets rid of mites. Do the job regularly in hot, dry weather, and make sure you get the undersides of leaves. Or spray with a solution of 1 teaspoon of nondetergent dishwashing liquid and 3 teaspoons of ammonia per 2½ gallons of water.

MOSAIC VIRUS

Symptoms include splotched, mottled, or puckered leaves and stunted growth. Remove and destroy affected tissue or the whole plant. Sterilize tools and wash your hands before touching healthy plants; plant resistant cultivars; control sap-sucking insects, especially aphids, which spread viruses.

RUST

Usually appears first as small orange or dark brown spots on undersides of leaves. The spots enlarge and spread rapidly, especially in damp or humid weather. Remove affected leaves, clean up debris, and spray once a week with this fungicide: in 1 gallon of water, combine 3 teaspoons of baking soda and either 1 teaspoon of nondetergent dishwashing liquid or 1 teaspoon of canola oil (but not both).

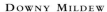

BEETLES, WEEVILS, AND BUGS

A multitude of these hard-bodied insects chew holes in leaves, stems, buds, petals, or fruits, sometimes transmitting diseases in the process. Handpick and drop the pests into a bucket of hot, soapy water. Alternatively, buy commercial traps or spray with soap and peppermint (see page 121). If you know the culprits are Japanese beetles, destroy the next generation (white grubs) by treating your lawn with milky spore disease, an otherwise harmless bacteria that kills several types of beetle grubs.

SLUGS AND SNAILS

Slugs and snails chew large, ragged holes in stems, flowers, and foliage—and leave behind their telltale silvery trails of slime. They're especially fond of citrus trees, hostas, and lettuce, but there are few plants they won't devour. Handpick them, and fasten a 1-inch band of copper around each container, just below the rim. Or sprinkle diatomaceous earth, wood ashes, sharp sand, or eggshells on the soil surface.

THRIPS

These all-but-invisible insects (about $\frac{1}{10}$ inch long) suck the juices from leaves, buds, flowers, and new growth tips. Affected leaf surfaces often look bronze or silvery with a pattern of dots where the chlorophyll has been siphoned off. Cut off and destroy infested plant parts (or toss the whole plant in the case of a badly damaged annual); release lacewings or entice wild ones; as a last resort, spray with insecticidal soap spray, either commercial or homemade (see page 121).

POWDERY MILDEW

Round white fungal spots appear on upper leaf surfaces, then expand until they merge into a gray or white powder on foliage and flowers (but not on woody parts). It is encouraged by poor air circulation, shade, and fog. Remove affected plant tissue; improve growing conditions; spray with a solution of 2 teaspoons each of baking soda and horticultural oil per gallon of water.

LEAF SPOTS

Many fungi and bacteria cause dark spots to develop on leaves. In most cases the damage is primarily cosmetic. Remove affected foliage immediately, keep containers and their surroundings free of plant debris, water early in the day, and avoid overhead watering.

MEALYBUGS

Sap-sucking insects leave white, fluffy wax and sticky honeydew; leaves spotted, distorted, or yellowed. Spray with a hose, and wash plants with soapy water (see "Scale").

SCALE

Scale appears as a bubbly, fuzzy, or crusty growth on leaves, stems, branches, and bark. Inside that crust, insects suck out plant juices, usually causing only cosmetic damage, with tissue looking sticky, rough, or spotted. Gently scrape off scale with a nail file; wash the plant with a solution of 2 teaspoons of nondetergent dishwashing liquid per gallon of water.

APHIDS (GREENFLIES)

These $\frac{1}{8}$-inch-long soft-bodied insects cluster primarily on new growth and suck out the sap, causing real damage only if they are present in great numbers. In most instances, a blast from a garden hose will solve the problem; in the case of severe infestation, use insecticidal soap or the soap and water spray on page 121. Ladybugs, the aphids' natural predator, provide long-term control.

CATERPILLARS AND WORMS

The larvae of numerous flying insects skeletonize leaves or chew holes in flowers, foliage, and fruit. Handpick; cover vegetable plants in spring to deter egg-laying adults (but remove covers when blossoms appear); spray with Bt.

Winterizing Your Garden

Unless you live in one of the country's warmest regions, your container plants will need protection from winter's chill. Some years, even in areas where potted plants can generally breeze through winter without missing a beat, Mother Nature might throw you a curve ball.

CHILLY WEATHER

At the first hint of a chill in the air—or when the weather forecast predicts dipping temperatures—move your pots to a protected place. Set them under a tree, carry them onto a covered porch, or haul them into the garage. In other words, do whatever you need to do to protect them from the open sky. If the containers are too heavy to move, use one or (better yet) all of the following tactics:

COVER THE PLANT Pound stakes in the ground or around the edges of the pot, and cover them with burlap, heavy plastic, a sheet or blanket, or (for smaller plants) a trash bag or cardboard box. If you use a box, cut off the bottom and slip the box over the plant; open the top flaps during the day to let in sunlight, and then close them at night.

INSULATE THE POT Wrap burlap sacks, blankets, or plastic bubble wrap around a container and tie it on with twine.

MULCH THE SOIL If you expect only a mild frost, a thick layer of straw, wood chips, or pine needles should give the roots all the protection they need.

CIRCLE THE WAGONS Draw pots close together for mutual protection and insulation.

Horticultural fleece (below left) and plastic bubble wrap (below right) provide excellent insulation from cold temperatures.

Protecting Pots

Containers, as well as plants, take a beating from freezing and thawing cycles. If possible, move your pots to shelter. Terra-cotta is particularly susceptible to damage, but even plastic can become brittle and crack when exposed to freezing temperatures (below).

If you have clay pots that you simply can't move indoors, try this: After digging up the plants, sink a 2-inch-wide shaft of plastic foam (from a hardware or craft store) down the center of the pot through the soil. When moisture in the soil freezes and expands, the foam will be compressed, taking pressure off the container walls.

REAL WINTER

In parts of the country where winter brings steady hard freezes, an outdoor container garden is a spring-to-fall pleasure only. Even the hardiest plant can't survive with its roots above ground in constant freezing or frequent below-zero temperatures. In these areas, if you want to grow anything but annuals, you have two choices:

MOVING INDOORS Tropical plants, with their year-round growing season, can carry on business as usual in a sunny south- or west-facing window. Plants that go dormant in winter can stay in a well-lighted garage or basement that doesn't freeze, or in an unheated room of the house. Deciduous plants can tolerate abrupt moves to a warmer area, but give evergreens some time in a transition zone, such as a protected porch, a spot below a deck, or a temporary shelter.

STAYING OUTDOORS Some hardy deciduous trees and shrubs, such as Japanese maples, hydrangeas, and roses, can be overwintered in their containers using a variant of the "Minnesota tip" method of protecting in-ground roses (presuming, of course, that you have soil to tip into). Once the plant has dropped all its leaves, dig a 10- to 12-inch-deep trench, and tip both container and plant over on their sides. Then cover both pot and plant with an 18- to 24-inch layer of leaves or straw, and top it off with a sheet of heavy plastic.

ABOVE: *Many herbs, as well as other plants, will winter cheerfully on a sunny windowsill. Shown here are parsley, sage, and golden marjoram.*

BELOW: *In places where winter is serious business, a gardener's best friend is a greenhouse. Catalogs and nurseries sell attractive versions that are small enough for many container-garden sites.*

Credits

PHOTOGRAPHY

B = bottom; L = left; M = middle; R = right; T = top; U = upper

A-Z Botanical Collection Ltd.: 13 B; **William D. Adams:** 33 T; **Max E. Badgley:** 120 TL; **Matthew Benson:** 9 TR, 58 B, 63 L, 66 TR; **Marion Brenner:** 9 TM, 10 T, 11 B, 12, 13 TL and TR, 13 ML and MR, 18 B, 24 all, 25 all, 37 T, 46 T and B, 47 L and R, 54 TL, 68 T and B, 69 L and R, 78 T and B, 82 T and B, 84 all, 85 all, 88 T, 89 B, 101 T, 101 M, 101 B, 109 T and B; **Roger Brooks/A-Z Botanical Collection Ltd.:** 73 T; **David Cavagnaro:** 38 R, 112 TL, 115 BR; **Robin B. Cushman:** 2 LM, 26, 34, 110, 113 TL; **Janet Davis:** 21 B, 30 T, 45, 112 UL; **Alan and Linda Detrick:** 83 B; **Andrew Drake/Garden Image:** 2 B, 29 T, 37 B, 48, 62 T; **Liz Eddison:** 31 B, 43 TR, 52 T, 55 B, 62 B, 95 T, 124 BR; **Derek Fell:** 100 T; **Roger Foley:** 75, 80 T; **John Glover:** 3 T, 8 B, 9 MR, 11 T, 16 L, 40 R, 53 BR, 60 L and R, 61 BR, 63 TR, 64 R, 65, 66 BL, 70, 72, 76 B, 80 B, 81 L, 99 B, 113 BL, 124 TR; **John Glover/Garden Picture Library:** 74 B; **David Goldberg:** 2 UM, 14, 36 B, 50 TL, 59 L, 66 BR; **Arthur Gray:** 100 B; **Steven Gunther:** 8 T, 17 T, 63 BR; **Jamie Hadley:** 57 TR, 114 T; 118; **Mick Hales:** 28 B; **Lynne Harrison:** 6 L, 17 BR, 35 L; **Saxon Holt:** 16 R, 29 B, 31 T, 32 T, 35 R, 41 T, 43 B, 57 BR, 58 T, 88 B, 89 T, 92; **Holt Studios/Nigel Cattlin:** 112 T and BR; **Holt Studios/Bob Gibbons:** 111 TR and BL; **Holt Studios/U. Kroner:** 126; **Holt Studios/John Veltom:** 23 B; **Dency Kane:** 40 L, 111 M, 112 LL and BL, 113 R, 115 TL; **Holt Studios/M. Szadzuik and R. Zinck:** 115 TM; **Allan Mandell:** 20 R, 30 B; **Charles Mann:** 20 L, 39 TL, 56, 64 BL; **David McDonald:** 6 R, 41 B, 51 B, 52 B; **Clive Nichols:** 1, 9 BL, 22 T, 32 B, 36 T, 39 TR and B, 50 BL, 53 T, 54 TR, 57 TL, 59 R, 61 T and BL, 66 TL, 73 B, 74 T, 125 T; **Marie O'Hara/Garden Picture Library:** 18 T; **Jerry Pavia:** 17 BL, 22 B, 23 L, 53 BL, 115 BL; **Julia Pazowski/A-Z Botanical Collection Ltd.:** 93 B; **Norman A. Plate:** 2 T, 4, 19 B, 28 T, 33 B, 44, 51 T, 54 B, 90, 91 T, 96 all, 97, 98, 99 T, 114 B; **Harry Smith Collection:** 125 B; **Thomas J. Story:** 3M and B, 9 BR, 10 B, 21 T, 23 R, 86, 91 B, 93 T, 94, 102, 104, 105 L and R, 106, 107, 116, 119 all; **Friedrich Strauss/Garden Picture Library:** 7, 38 L, 83 T, 95 B, 124 BL; **Ron Sutherland/Garden Picture Library:** 55 T, 76 T, 81 R; **Bjorn Svensson/A-Z Botanical Collection Ltd.:** 19 T; **Mark Turner:** 42, 43 TL, 111 TL and BR, 112 UR and LR, 115 TR; **Ron West:** 120 BL, BR, TR; **Steven Wooster/Garden Picture Library:** 64 TL.

DESIGN

Bill and Dana Anderson: 63 BR; **Mark Ashmead:** 40 R; **Jonathan Baillie:** 60 L; **Rob Benoit Associates:** 21 T; **Susan Blevins:** 64 BL; **Kathleen N. Brenzel:** 88 B, 89 T, 91 T; **Susanna Brown:** 62 B; **Ralph Cade/Robin Greene:** 22 T, 36 T, 53 T; **Natalie Charles:** 43 TR; **Stephen Crisp:** 74 B, 76 B; **Robin B. Cushman:** 113 TL; **Scott Daigre:** 100 B; **Tina Dixon:** 28 T, 30 B, 33 B; **Ann Frith:** 53 BR; **Teena Garay:** 90; **Sonny Garcia:** 29 B; **John Glover:** 99 B; **Karen Guzak:** 35 L; **Ben Hammontree:** 41 B; **Mark Henry:** 52 B; **Tom Hobbs:** 6 R; **Lynn Hollyn:** 3M, 86, 94 (concrete containers); **Raquel Hughes:** 20 L; **Chris Jacobson:** 9 BR, 43 B; **Ann Kelly:** 42; **Joan Kropf:** 34; **Land Art:** 61 BR; **Randy Lancaster:** 19 B; **Stonie Lewenhaupt:** 66 TL; **Little & Lewis Design:** 17 BR; **Emma Lush:** 39 TR; **Jean Manocchio:** 44; **Patti McGee:** 51 B; **Callie McRoskey:** 59 L; **Claire Mee/Candy Bros.:** 54 TR; **Carol Mercer/Lisa Verderosa:** 40 L; **Clive and Jane Nichols:** 57 TL, 61 T and BL; **Oehme, van Sweden & Associates:** 75, 80 T; **Anthony Paul:** 55 T, 72, 81 R; **Ellen Pearce:** 36 B; **Lisette Pleasance:** 50 BL; **Suzanne Porter:** 18 B; **Nan Raymond:** 39 TL, 56; **Sarah Robertson:** 2 LM, 26; **Charlotte Sanderson:** 59 R; **Hilda Schwerin:** 99 T; **Candra A. Scott:** 2 UM, 14; **Randle Siddeley:** 74 T; **Jill Slater:** 3M (plants) and B, 9 TM, 11 B, 24 B; 25 all, 46 B, 47 L and R, 68 B, 69 L and R, 84 B, 85, 86 (plants), 88 T, 89 B, 91 B, 93 T, 94 (plants), 101, 102; **Jill Slater/Jan Smith:** 37 T; **Billy Spratlin:** 17 T; **Robert and Judith Stitzel:** 43 TL; **Stonesmith Garden Vessels:** 91 T (container); **Diana Stratton:** 32 T; **Bud Stuckey:** 23 R, 98; **Martin Summers:** 64 TL; **Joe Swift:** 9 BL; **Bernard Trainor:** 50 TL; **Greg Trutza:** 51 T; **Ron Wagner/Nani Waddoups:** 20 R; **Tisa Watts:** 54 B; **Geoff Whitten:** 39 B; **Paul Williams:** 18 T; **Stephen Woodhams:** 1, 32 B, 73 B, 125 T; **Kay Yamada:** 31 B.

Index

Page numbers in **boldface** refer to photographs.